THIS

is Africa 2

More True Tales of a Safari Guide

ISBN: 1500830933
ISBN 13: 9781500830939
Library of Congress Control Number: 2014914551
CreateSpace Independent Publishing Platform
North Charleston, South Carolina

This book is dedicated to:

*All those who fight the good fight for the future
of all creatures, great and small*

*Lovers of Africa who understand that to be a lover,
one must be a fighter*

*My family and friends, who must know that Africa
could not mean a hundredth as much to me as it does
without your love and support*

*And, of course, George and Hope,
my two greatest inspirations*

TABLE OF CONTENTS

INTRODUCTION

It has been two years since *THIS is Africa: True Tales of a Safari Guide* went to print, and I am still "following my heart" in Africa as Barry suggested to me eight years ago. I still had many stories to tell but no time to sit and write them. My company, TIA Safaris, has kept me busier in the business realm than I had hoped. It has forced me to spend at least half of the last four years since its inception in the United States rather than in my beloved Africa. The benefits have been that I have had a great deal of privilege and opportunity in lecturing to schools, colleges, religious institutions, and organizations from the Audubon Society to Rotary Clubs about Africa, its glorious wildlife, people, and its trials and tribulations. Although nothing is better than being in Africa, sharing Africa with people in any form is always a joy and honor.

In looking back at some of the stories from my past that I used to write in email form, which makes up a portion of this book, I came across something I wrote as heartfelt and honestly as anything I have ever written. Although it was written for a very specific event, missing my graduation from Ulovane Environmental Training on Amakhala Game Reserve in South Africa in 2007, there is something undeniably universal about its spirit and its message that made me want to put it here in the introduction to this book. It could be extended to all those I have met and with whom I have shared Africa in the almost seven years following my life-changing stay on Amakhala.

Everyone,

I first want to convey to everyone how saddened I am by my inability to be here with you tonight. It most certainly would have been one of the best of my life, being able to celebrate with all you wonderful people the completion of a year that has somehow already come to an end. Unfortunately, the future is already pulling me away from what was undoubtedly the best year of my life. Aside from being here on Amakhala, one of the most beautiful places on the planet, it was living, learning, and working with you all that made my year a privilege, an honor, and a dream come true.

I have spent most of my life alone in my endeavors. Playing tennis, traveling the world, and writing scripts were solitary exercises that required a great deal of sacrifice from what most would consider a normal life, and, more often than not, the rewards were enjoyed alone. What being here with all of you has meant to me is therefore worth infinitely more than anything I have put my heart and soul into previously. Every moment I have spent here, I have had the privilege of sharing it with you all. I never could have imagined how much I enjoyed being part of a team, a family, an idea, a vision, here with such extraordinary people in such an extraordinary place. I had often wondered what it would be like to be a part of a team, working toward a common goal, with a common vision. Now I can only wonder at how much I may have missed in my past, having seen what a team and a family truly are here on Amakhala.

When we first arrived here at Ulovane, we all sat in a circle to introduce ourselves, tell our histories, tell how we came to be here, and what we expected from being here. Afterward, Schalk astutely said how wonderful it was that we, who had arrived from all over the world, from different backgrounds, with different goals and dreams, yet with a common love of nature, could all end up in the same place. What I have loved most about being here is indeed the host of characters making up the memories. I could spend the whole night recounting special moments that I shared with each of you that will happily filter through my memory banks for the rest of my life, but I'm sure there isn't enough alcohol, tissue, or time here for that so I'll move straight through to the "thank yous."

Schalk and Candice, Chris and Erica, how can I thank you enough for creating a program and imbuing it with your hearts and souls. It has not only enriched my education and helped me fulfill a dream, but has also deepened my understanding of how to be a better person. You have taught me to unveil the beauty in things that could not previously be seen or known, to be smart and perceptive in ways that will abet me every step of my way. Most thankfully, you have shown me new ways in which to love the world that I had not imagined possible. I leave here forever in your debt for the wealth of knowledge, experience, and joy I have garnered. You have made your own dream a reality. Thank you, thank you, and thank you…

To my fellow field guides and Raz and Natalie, I must first offer my apologies. I apologize if I inadvertently sent you to see giraffe who weren't northwest of Flokkie's Vlei when, in fact, it was rhino southeast of Englovu Pan. I apologize for every Xhosan animal name that I massacred with my totally incomprehensible pronunciation. Lastly I apologize for taking up the airwaves calling in creatures that most of you, and certainly your guests, would cheerfully DOOM if, in fact, you actually came across the animal. Please know I tried my best as much for your sakes as my own. Be that as it may, I thank you all for supporting me and each other in a very high pressure, potentially dangerous, and exhausting occupation that we all love so much. I hope everywhere I go my coworkers and colleagues are as professional, fun-loving, clever, and have as profound a love of the environment as do all of you. It has been an undeniable honor being out there in the trenches with you all, and I will miss your smiling faces behind the Landie's steering wheels every time I think of this place. I will not, however, miss the Paterson Pub as much as you all will. It's funny how your faces at the Pub were decidedly different than when behind the Landie's wheels (most of the time anyway), which is probably a damn good thing...

I want to send a special thanks to "Rhino Andy," certainly the Second Degree of Separation for most, if not all of us, in so many searches for our needed sightings. Being our "Eye in the Sky," you were an indispensable part of our every game drive when you were out there on the reserve. I actually considered telling my guests we weren't allowed to go out until you came back from wherever you went off to on your breaks. We and our guests are indebted to you for a thousand different sightings.

My fellow Ulovaneans, we have laughed, cried, studied our asses off together, and created lifelong bonds for which I cannot begin to express my gratitude. Whenever I struggled, you were there to support me. If I thought myself too smart, you were there to humble me with a greater wisdom. You challenged me with your intellect, your fortitude, and your determination. You inspired me with your dedication and your infinitely good humor at times when it would have been much better to bawl our eyes out. Ben, I thank you for your tutelage, your wisdom, your boundless generosity, and your hilarity. Although many of us are scarred for life from your bodily function jokes, you were always everyone's most helpful friend and an inspiration on how one should live this life. At Ulovane, I could not have hoped for a better bunch of people than you to fill the spaces offered. I love you guys...

To the Landowners of Amakhala and particularly the Fowld's family. I thank you for having the courage, the determination, the will, and the vision to create and sustain this unforgettable reserve and let us all be a part of it. My dream could not have been fulfilled without your own dream. I could not have hoped for a more magnificent place as the setting for my dream's fruition. Like countless guests have said to me, being here on Amakhala was the best time of their lives. It may have had something to do with Uncle Bill keeping them up until 2:00 in the morning and still being drunk at 6:00 for drives. But since I don't drink, and I had the best time of MY life, it was probably more likely the beauty and wonder of your reserve that made it so. May you and Amakhala thrive and prosper over the years and all its denizens live happy, healthy lives under the fascinated and admiring eyes of generations to come.

Lastly I want to thank George and the creatures here who gave me the greatest fleeting moments of my whole life. They taught me, above all other things, to love the beauty and wonder of our lives, while we have it before us right here and now. They emblazoned on my heart the reminder that to those of us who wish to be stewards of the Earth, because of our love of nature, it will never be an easy love, crystal-fragile at its best moments, and heartbreaking at its worst. I am filled with the magic that will forever provide me the strength and courage to share nature's wonder with all those I meet in my future in this industry.

The best of things to you all,
Mat

I am endlessly grateful for all that being a safari guide has given me and allowed me to give to anyone who would share Africa and all its wonders with me. Being a safari guide has allowed me the privilege of sharing what is best and most wonderful about being a *being* on planet Earth. It has taught me the true meaning of *connection*. I hope this book, like my first, will inspire those desiring to come to Africa to make the journey and for those who have already been, to come back on safari.

I also hope those who find the magic of Africa in these pages realize that visiting Africa, the home from which all peoples originate, is not a right but a privilege of privileges. Africa and its remarkable denizens, with all their seemingly timeless survivability, have a fragile future that will be undoubtedly solidified by the conscientious patronage of Africa, by investment, charitable contributions, and/ or, of course, by visiting this most beautiful of continents.

Mat Dry, 2014

CHAPTER ONE

ELEPHANT CONNECTIONS

AS GOOD AS IT GETS

L ooking down at her, I am stumped as to what I should do. She lies with her mouth slightly open, her thick hair falling across her cheek and shoulder. She looks beautiful in the full moon's residual light within the tent, peaceful and serene. If I wake her and show her at what I've been looking at, I'm pretty confident that serenity is going to be wrecked. In fact, Kay might just freak out completely. We can't have that. *They might go away*.

I check my watch for the time: 3:08 in the morning here in the Okavango Delta. I am wide awake after hearing the loud cracking of branches that can only be one thing when out in the wilds of Africa. *Elephants*. I peer out again at the huge bull standing with his two bachelor herd buddies in the light of the full moon not forty yards from the mesh of our tent. Another cracking, like the one that woke me, resounds in the still night air. He and his pals are pulling whole branches off the trees and stripping them of leaves and bark. It's so loud I'm amazed she doesn't wake up. I listen for the stirring of my other clients as they lie in their respective tents twenty yards to our right. Nothing. *Good. I won't need to yell to them to stay in their tents in case they are thinking of getting up for a middle of the night toilet visit*.

Should I wake her, should I not wake her? Aye, that is the question. I weigh the options in my head. Kay is a very brave and strong woman but it was not without trepidation that she came to the Delta, like many of my clients. The Delta can be very intimidating especially when one hears stories of dugout canoes being overturned by submerged hippos, lions and hyenas having pulled people away from the campsite who had chosen not to sleep near a fire or in a tent, and a place where elephants may very well wander through the campsite if the fire isn't still burning brightly. *Like tonight.*

I watch and listen to them munching away in the ghostly light of the forest for two minutes. I can't help but smile, not just on my face, but from the very depth of my being. This is why I am alive, to be at peace with nature and its proudest representatives. A wave of privilege and gratefulness sweeps over me, and I realize it would be a crime not to share it with Kay. I lean down and gently cover her mouth.

"Shhhh. Sorry to wake you, but I don't want you to miss this."

Her huge blue eyes shoot open and stare into mine with momentary fear. It shifts to a trusting curiosity.

"You just have to be very quiet and make as little movement as possible."

She nods beneath my hand. "What is it?" she asks with childlike fascination.

I help sit her up, and we lean toward the entrance of the tent. I point to the huge bodies moving in trees. It is amazing how easy it is to see them in the moonlight. Her eyes widen, and she looks back at me with genuine excitement. I smile and raise my eyebrows. *Good times!* Two of the bulls move deeper into the forest leaving the biggest bull idling where I first saw him.

"Amazing, huh?" I wrap my arm around her and whisper, "This is as good as it gets." *Or is it?*

It occurs to me how on several occasions in the past I had sent "telepathic" messages to elephants, and they had come over to me. The most amazing one being the first time I tried with George, our second biggest bull on Amakhala Game Reserve, after my second week of being there. That turned out to be the most amazing moment of my life. I can't explain it, but the fact it has happened several times makes me think telepathy with these amazing creatures is possible. *How amazing would it be to share that with Kay if this were actually true?* I question the sanity of it and laugh to myself. I must be nuts to think that elephants are telepathic. I decide to give it another try.

I lean forward slightly and focus on the elephant idly munching in the moonlight. I begin my mantra in my head, *Please come. Please come. Please come...* One minute goes by. Two minutes go by. I don't stop my mantra. I am thinking that this elephant and I are connected by some unseen force and that he will come over to us when he feels it. I make it the core of my being and send my invitation to the elephant. *We are connected. We are connected.*

I am wondering if Kay can feel anything from me as the bull turns from his demolished tree and faces us. A burst of joy lights me up inside. *Is it even possible?* He begins to walk toward us. Tingles around my face force a huge grin. I turn to Kay just in case this pachyderm has indeed heeded my telepathic invitation.

"If he comes over don't worry. Don't say anything. Don't move. It will be fine. We are fine in here. The tent is just like a big, human-smelling rock, okay?" She looks at me with her luminous eyes filled with fear, but she trusts me. She nods at me, and I smile to reassure her. We both look back at the elephant. He rounds another clump of trees thirty yards out where there are plenty of delicious trees to browse from. He doesn't stop there.

That's right, buddy. Keep coming. We would love to see you close up. The slight crunch of leaves is the only sound the bull makes as he beelines toward our tent. Thirty yards, twenty-five yards, twenty yards, he languidly strides toward us. He reaches a fallen tree fifteen yards from the front of our tent. This, I think, will be the true test of whether or not he truly has "heard" my telepathic message. Between us and the fallen tree there is nothing but a small bush. It is one foot high, four feet across, and ten feet from our faces. He couldn't possibly have passed all that foliage and trees to feed off of that. He wouldn't have even seen it there from his original spot.

Kay sucks in a deep breath as the bull rounds the end of the fallen tree. I hug her to me and put a finger over my mouth. "Close your eyes if you're scared. He won't hurt us I promise," I barely whisper. I'm quite certain Kay's heart is doing the exact thing as my own. There is thunder in my chest as the gargantuan pachyderm strides toward us. *Holy sh-t, he IS coming over to us!*

From our seated perspective on the ground, it seems like he rises up before us. He is *ENORMOUS.* There is nothing but ELEPHANT in our eyes. All of a sudden, my confidence wanes. I have no idea the extent to which or how telepathy works, if it works at all. In the past I have always verbally spoken to the elephants when they have come over to me. I can't possibly say anything aloud to the elephant this close and from the tent. A talking tent might cause a one-elephant stampede. *Stop.* I send the message to him as he steps up to the little bush that would be the only thing between us and him. Unbelievably, (or believably) he does. The bull stands there at the bush as if waiting for something to happen. I am flabbergasted. I hadn't thought this far ahead. The rational me thinks, *What the hell does this elephant want with that little bush when he could be eating the entire forest around us?* My fear has made me doubt my telepathic connection with this huge animal.

Neither Kay nor I can move. We have been enormously rewarded by either my telepathic messaging or just the universe itself. To be ten feet from the foot of the largest land animal in the world is a privilege of privileges, and I am astounded, in awe, trapped in wonder. As if not knowing himself why he is standing there, he drops his trunk to the little bush and begins picking at it with the two fingers at the tip of his trunk. He picks at the leaves and idly brings them to his mouth like we would with our fingers and crumbs of bread. It is absurd and awesome at the same time. He can rip down whole trees with his trunk or pick tiny leaves from a meager bush. I want to scream with joy but at the same time I am starting to be uncomfortable with him being this close to us.

I can feel the fear emanating from Kay next to me. I don't blame her. He is a juggernaut before us. I know if someone decided to come out of his or her tent from the campsite twenty yards to our right, it may give him a reason to trundle over the tent and into the woods, leaving us strawberry jam behind him. I begin a new mantra in my head. *Thank you, my friend. Thank you for coming over here. Thank you for sharing you with us. Go now. Please go and thank you for sharing with us.* I say this for over a minute as he picks uninterestedly at the little bush. If I did call him over here, he definitely didn't get the better deal of this midnight connection.

Kay grabs my arm, and I jump as someone unzips a tent in the campsite to our right. *Holy sh-t! Not now! Not now*! I scream in my head. I look up to the bull, and his ears shoot open. He turns his massive head to face the noise. If he was a world in our eyes before, he is *everything* now.

Kay folds into a ball in my arm and sucks in her breath yet again. I crush her to me, and the lightning fast debate rushes to my head. *Do I scream and tell them to stay in their tent and risk scaring the elephant where he might charge us OR stay quiet and wait to see if the person emerging from the tent will do what I told him or her to do when coming out from the tent at night and will instantly see the enormous elephant standing no more than twenty yards from him or her?*

I stare at the elephant before us, my heart thundering in my chest. I have never in my life had to sit still with this much adrenaline in my system. I feel like I could lift off into orbit. Kay is a shivering ball next to me. I'm quite certain her eyes are sealed shut but I'm not checking. My eyes are filled with elephant but my ears are straining to hear if anyone is getting out of the tent. The person is rummaging around the tent for a flashlight I imagine, as no light has beamed in any direction that my peripheral vision can pick up. I decide to send some telepathy my client's way. *Stay in your tent, stay in your tent, stay in your tent*...I only hear more rummaging.

The elephant raises his trunk to smell in the direction of the tent. I can see he is deciding whether he should cut and run or get ready to attack. *Go, go, go, go, go*...I send to him. If he hears me, he doesn't show it. I'm pretty sure if my client gets out of his tent there will be a charge.

The zipper rips the silence again. It is like the sharpest fingernails on the biggest chalkboard I've ever heard. Apparently it sounds the same to the elephant. With a small head shake, the bull swivels his bulk on his axis, his butt to the campsite. I hear my passenger climbing from the tent but can't scream yet. *Just wait, just wait, just wait*...I cram my head against the screen and watch the bull starting to stride away. One step, two step, three step he disappears from my vision, and I flip to the window just to my right. "*Stay in your tent!*" I hiss as loudly as I can.

I see Doug, a fifty-something teacher from Canada, standing at his tent about to zip it back up before he goes off to the toilet.

"What is it!" he yells.

"Elephant! Stay there until I say it's okay to get out!" I say. I watch him dive his tall, gawky frame into the dark interior of his tent with the alacrity of a mongoose.

"Forget it!" he yells, zipping his tent back up. "I'll hold it to morning!"

I laugh out loud, releasing the pent-up adrenaline. I look out our left window and see the huge rear-end of the bull disappearing into the leaves of the trees twenty yards out. He is done with us. I peer down at Kay who is looking up at me with her eyes, pools of fear.

"It's okay. He's gone." She is speechless, her mouth working to say something, anything. "How's that for a close encounter?" I ask.

"Oh, my Gawd!" is all she can say. I laugh and hug her.

"Oh…MY…*GAWWWD!*" she repeats in case I missed the memo.

"*That*," I say. "*THAT* is as good as it gets."

AN ELEPHANT POODLE

"Check that out," Andy says, handing me the binoculars. He points in the distance to the limestone road writhing up the hill a mile from us. I look into the binos toward where he is pointing. A fifth the way up the hill, three elephants wrestle in the trees just to the right of the road. "Who is it you think?" I ask. "Hard to tell," he says. "It looks like the smaller ones." I nod and hand my binos to the couple behind us.

Jan and Anita are a young, thirty-something couple from Amsterdam. They are the epitome of soft-spoken and unassuming. In fact they are so soft-spoken and unassuming, I have had to turn around a few times to see if they are still there at all. At the numerous sightings we've already had of the rhinos, several antelope species, and giraffe on this drive around Amakhala, they met our enthusiastic explanations with blinking eyes and barely perceptible nodding. I'm hoping elephants will get them going.

"You guys want to see some elephants wrestling?" I ask animatedly. Jan has his arm wrapped around Anita's shoulder. They both move their shoulders slightly. I take it as a huge statement of enthusiasm on their part. "Great. Let's go, my man," I say to Andy.

We have to travel a rather circuitous route to get to where the elephants are having it out on the hill. Along the way we explain the significance of elephants "fighting."

"Throughout their lives, male elephants will wrestle with other male elephants in order to bond as well as learn the techniques they will need in the future to battle for the right to breed with females. Many people misperceive this wrestling as fighting and watch for one of the elephants to kill the other. Even when the elephants are truly fighting, killing is very rare. Most elephant solve their dominance issues with the simple establishment of who is larger and thus more powerful."

The couple looks at me, unblinking. I slip back in my seat trying to remember if the couple speaks English or not. I give Andy a sidelong look, and he snickers. Not everyone gives two shakes of an elephant's trunk about elephant behavior, or any animal behavior for that matter. It's enough that Andy and I do.

As we hit the road leading to the white of the limestone road we can see the elephants through the trees. They are having a grand 'ole time. It is Macauley, seventeen, Biliki, thirteen, and Afsterdt (Tailless) who is just nine. After our second largest bull, George, twenty-five, died several months before from electrocution, these are our third to sixth largest male elephants on the reserve. It is wonderful to see Macauley assuming a role that George or Norman, our dominant bull, would usually assume. I explain this to our illustrious couple as Andy chugs the vehicle toward the mouth of the road leading up to the combatants.

"Male elephants are allowed to remain in their natal head with their mothers, sisters, and aunts until about puberty. This is because they will then try and mate with the females in the herd, most of whom are their relatives. Thus, the females will tolerate them until the danger of inbreeding becomes a reality. The young males are pushed farther and farther away from the herd until they are booted for good. They will be allowed to return to the herd for visiting as long as they behave themselves. This process can be quite emotional for the young males as they are being excluded from what has been a tight-knit family for the first dozen or so years of their lives."

I look back to see if the couple will respond in the usual way people respond when they hear about the "kicking out" of the young males. Most respond with an "Awwww, that's so sad" or something similar. They are looking at me as if waiting for something more. I take that as a good sign and continue, looking at them. "The process is made easier by the young males joining up with other males to form what we call bachelor herds, like this one we see here." I jab my thumb back over my shoulder. "They will join up with other males, very much as teenagers, until they come into musth, a heightened state of testosterone, which indicates they are ready to mate. After that, they will spend more time alone than in the company of others." I finish, hoping we have reached the elephants. I turn back around to see where we are in relation to them. We *are* the elephants. Andy has chugged us right up alongside the pachyderm pugilists.

Having been in the same school with Andy and being trained by the same teachers, I would have thought that he had the same ideas about approaching the elephants in their mood, on a limestone road that goes up at a rather steep angle, and with trees on both sides of the road. In the event of agitation, no one is going anywhere in our logistical setting here, especially us.

There are several things to understand before entering into any animal sighting, particularly sightings of the larger and more dangerous ones. Most important, of course, is to judge the animals' behavior: Are they excited or agitated? Are they feeding, mating, or otherwise feeling vulnerable to attack? Are they staring at you with an alert expression or hostile attitude? The next thing to consider after deciding whether or not to approach the animal is the logistics.

One only wants to approach the sighting if there is both a way in and a way out for both you and the animal. This is in case the animals become agitated during the sighting and being there for you is no longer "peaches and sunshine." I would have placed the car at the bottom of the hill and watched the elephants duke it out from thirty yards away. Andy had decided to take the adventuresome path and drove us *right* up to where the three elephants are fighting. Apparently, he is going to get the Dutch couple riled up one way or another.

Afsterdt, used to being in the comfort of the herd and not the bachelor herd, decides our being there is too much for him. He swivels his two-ton bulk into a small tree and crushes it. He opens his ears and stands there to watch how his two elephant brothers handle our green machine in their midst. Macauley and Biliki don't pay any attention to us and continue pressing their tusks against each other.

As Afsterdt takes his place in the tree line, Biliki tries to push Macauley backward toward us. The largest male in any of the wrestling groups will sometimes allow the smaller elephants to dominate them if only perhaps to encourage the smaller ones to continue their battling. It would be counterproductive for the species if the larger males kept defeating the young ones with every move. Andy smiles broadly at me as Macauley's butt reaches ten yards from us. I have to pull myself together to keep from yelling out the list of things I feel he has done wrong so far with this sighting. I don't, mostly because I don't want to scare the bejeezus out of the clients. I turn back to them.

"Guys, please be as quiet as possible, stay in the middle of the vehicle, and if the animals approach just stay silent and still. Okay?" They nod at me without expression. All I can think as I look at them is at least I won't have to worry about them freaking out like some might when the larger animals approach the vehicle. We may as well be watching tortoises racing as impressed as they seem to be.

Sitting completely still next to battling elephants, even if they are only wrestling, however, is unsettling to say the least. At least I am unsettled. The couple behind us has no fear in their eyes, just a gentle amusement as if they were watching a circus elephant show. I'm happy as they are not aware of our potentially hazardous placement in the universe at the moment.

The clacking of the tusks as they press their bulk against one another, the scratching of their skin as they turn their shoulders into one another, and the expelling of their breath as they grunt and heave themselves is almost palpable to us watching the elephants. I peek at Andy to see what he's thinking. I can't help but feel forgiving toward him as the look on his face expresses exactly why we do this job. He, like me, loves this stuff. I settle down for a moment and just enjoy the show.

After two minutes of sitting here, it is apparent the elephants are treating us as just another part of the scenery. That is a good thing. We have passed their comfort zone test. That, however, creates another issue: If they are undisturbed by our proximity, because they see us as just another thing in there vicinity, nothing will stop them from pushing each other *into* us. As I consider this prospect, Biliki gives Macauley, whose butt is facing us, a head shake, meaning he is ready to get down and dirty with him. Macauley, in his big brotherly way, gives him a head shake of his own but stands his ground. Biliki decides to move forward in a little charge.

Now usually this wouldn't be an issue at all for Macauley. Just his sheer weight could keep Biliki from going anywhere. Macauley, however, takes Biliki on the head, the crack of their tusks ricocheting across the plain below us, and backs up. In response he places his trunk on Biliki's head. This is a sign of dominance and usually signifies that he has already had it with the sparring. Biliki stops for a moment feeling the trunk on his head and then starts pushing again. If they had been humans, Macauley would be the big brother holding the little brother's head out away from him as the little brother swings away at his unreachable torso.

As amusing as it is to us and Macauley, it isn't so amusing to Biliki. He lets out a small *hurrumph* and then pushes with all his might against his much larger foe. Macauley decides to humor Biliki and allows him to push him. The only problem, of course, is that we are ten yards directly behind Macauley's rear. If Macauley presses against us, he could easily crush that side of the vehicle and cause it flip over with all of us in it. Macauley allows Biliki to push him closer, and closer, and closer. At five yards, Andy and I both start talking. "Hey, Macauley we're right here behind you, buddy! Watch out Macauley, we're right here!"

Hearing us, Macauley spins around like a gigantic ballet dancer and opens his ears. It is an awesome display. With his ears open, his head from ear to ear seems easily as wide as our vehicle is long. We don't let it bother us. "Hey buddy. We've just come to see you guys wrestling. Don't mind us. You're doing just fine without us," we babble to him.

He considers us for a good ten seconds and decides that we are as uninteresting as apparently wrestling with his minors is. He turns sideways to the vehicle facing uphill, now arm's length from Andy's head. He looks at us with his long-lashed eye and listens as we continue our litany of pleasantries. After another ten seconds, he's had enough. He starts his way uphill.

When his rear reaches the windshield, the loose skin around his rear aperture flaps crazily. An enormous *POODLEPOODLEPOODLE* sound rushes from Macauley accompanied by the horrible stench of a five-ton herbivore.

"Ah, maaannn!" Andy says, one hand covering his nose and mouth. "That's disgusting!"

I cover my own nose and mouth and stifle a laugh. One would think the true king of the jungle would have a sonorous blast that could be heard from miles around not this poodlepoodling. Even the Dutch couple covers their faces. I giggle. Not everybody gets the privilege of being wafted by elephant flatus.

Andy sees me out of the corner of his eye. He turns to me and then to the couple with the earnestness of a teacher reprimanding his students and says, "Don't laugh! Don't laugh!" Even if I wasn't going to laugh, his histrionics are too much for what little self control I have. I open my mouth to let out a guffaw and immediately shove my knuckle in my mouth. The laugh I have brewing is not going to be appreciated by Macauley this close to us.

I bite on my finger enough to cause me considerable pain. Andy shakes his finger at me. "Don't you laugh! Don't you laugh!" The couple behind us is actually smiling, more from the tears popping into my eyes and my face turning red than from the poodling that continues unabated as Macauley's butt reaches the front of the Land Rover. Andy eyes me seriously and points. "It's not funny," he says. That cuts it for me. I burst out laughing. So does Andy.

"Ha, ha, ha, ha!" We laugh, tears shooting from our eyes. I cough and sputter. Macauley, now directly in front of the vehicle, spins around toward us. He lets off an angry trumpet and spreads his massive ears. He raises his trunk over the hood of the Land Rover. If he brings it down, he could crush the engine into the ground through the hood. Andy and I both cut our laughter off completely.

"It's okay, buddy," I offer. "It's all right! EVERYBODY does that! It's not your fault! We weren't laughing at you. We're sorry!" I can't even hear what Andy is saying through my apologetic diatribe. Macauley listens to us, turning his head slightly left and slightly right to consider our apology in stereo to him. He can tell by the tone of our voices that not only are we sorry, but also the stupid noises we make at his flatus are no danger to him.

It is a tense ten seconds as we continue apologizing and softening our tones. We successfully reassure him. With one last head shake, he drops his trunk. He turns himself uphill and strides determinedly away. As he continues up the road from us, the poodle-poodling continues. I can't help but laugh. Andy wipes a tear from his face and turns to our illustrious couple. "What'd you think of that?" He laughs.

"Big and smelly," Anita says emphatically. Jan smiles widely and nods at that. I am pleased to see they have actually enjoyed something of their game drive experience. After all, it is not everyday one gets a close encounter with an elephant poodle.

OUT OF THE DARKNESS
AND INTO THE LIGHT

I am in a foul mood when I disembark from our truck at Namutoni Fort, deep within Etosha National Park, Namibia. Already six o'clock, it has been a long day of driving from our previous campsite, followed by game driving within Etosha. Usually people can become quite restless during the day from all the driving. Usually the amazing creatures in Etosha make the last hours on the truck worth the whole while. Not today. Today has been a nightmare of rudeness, cantankerousness, and general chaos on the truck. Usually none of that bothers me.

Today is different for a number of reasons. Paradoxically, it is mostly because I genuinely like everyone on board individually. The majority of the group, however, despite the fact that I genuinely like every one of them, have proven to be a pain in my and the other third's proverbial neck. The dynamic this majority has created is one where they constantly have to one-up each other. If one person makes a joke, someone else has to one-up that joke and around and around it goes, even if I am in the middle of imparting important information. Over the past several weeks it has become exhausting, and worse, it angers the other minority who want to listen and learn. Ten days earlier, I actually had to warn one of the majority of the group that if he repeated his shenanigans of late-night carousing, I would have to kick him off the truck. The truth is, sometimes, even in Africa, I have my dark days.

I decide to eschew the workout I usually do when I reach Namutoni and head straight to the water hole. Like many resorts within wild places, particularly in Etosha, there is a lighted water hole where guests can go, relax with a libation, and wait all night, if necessary, for animals to come and join them. Some resorts have a borehole that bubbles water up for this purpose. Namutoni's has a natural spring and is the original reason the fort was built in this location. This being the case, there is also a great deal of vegetation there within the water as well as along it.

A vast hedge of common reed grows alongside the fence and one side of the huge fort. This harbors thousands of weavers and waterbirds as well as acting as a refuge for smaller mammals. The water hole even has fish in it, which can be seen splashing in the shallows from time to time. It is a wonderful place to watch the sunset, see nocturnal animals, and rejuvenate from tough days on the road. It is also a place where Africa's most mythical creatures may be found in their greatest glory.

The black sky has a deep red strip on the horizon as I walk up the boardwalk to the huge gazebo overlooking the water hole. Thankfully, there is no one else sitting in the benches beneath the gazebo's beautifully thatched roof. The huge flood lamp illuminates the water hole in a ghostly brilliance. The chirping of the weavers settling in for the night among the reeds is almost deafening as they join in chorus with the reed frogs that call Namutoni home. I look at the benches and decide not to sit there. I don't want to see another person for at least another hour until I finish communing with nature.

I move off to the left and to the front of the gazebo, much closer to the reeds and to far left of the spotlight. I climb up on one of the five-foot pillars that hold the horizontal poles that make up the first fence just this side of the electric one. The electric fence is there to prevent any potentially dangerous animals from entering into the fort proper. I sit and cross my legs.

I contemplate why I am so frustrated with the majority of the group. They are really just trying to have a good time on a trip that can be quite taxing in terms of hours spent on the truck. I'm also more than used to people not being interested in the unending factoids and in-depth analysis about everything we see in Africa's wild places, the information that makes me love these creatures and their homes. I even come with a disclaimer, which I offer during every predeparture meeting: "I will be offering a constant stream of information about things we see, places we visit, people we meet, and creatures we find. At some point you may even want to stuff a sock in my mouth as I go on *ad nauseum*. None of what I say are you required to listen to. It is there to give you a greater understanding of Africa as you adventure through it." So why now with this group?

I realize it is because this information is given not only for sharing the beauty and wonder of Africa with people, but more importantly because I know these wild places with their extraordinary inhabitants are living extremely fragile existences. They are reliant almost entirely on people like the ones in my group, people who make the effort to come to Africa and experience the wildness. The sad truth is that these wild places will not survive without the patronage of tourists. These animals and peoples that call these places home require people *to be interested* in them if they are going to survive the onslaught of "progress" and industry. In the most simple terms, if these people aren't impressed with the wonder and beauty of these places, there is no impression that will be made when they return home to describe their experience to family and friends. The legacy of interest will cease as will the future of these places I love. I know this group has the capacity to understand this and their flippancy and disregard is thus doubly hard to take.

Perhaps, ultimately, it is my foolish assumption that once people experience and learn about something bigger and greater than themselves, they cannot help want to preserve that which carries so much wonder and beauty. I realize my job isn't about changing people's minds or even opening their hearts to these places. In the end, I am here being a safari guide for me, these places, and the people who do want to know about these treasures. It has to be enough that *we* are infused with the wonder and beauty and that there are a precious few who will take Africa into their hearts and minds.

I am not a meditative person but I decide to concentrate on my breathing and focus on the noises and smells around me. The roar of the birds in the reeds mixes with the chorus of the frogs. I can hear a nightjar screeching as it hawks insects in the heat of the light. I hear the flapping of bat wings as they fly by just above me, catching insects. I sit like this for an untold time, breathing. I think of myself as a part of, and connected to, the darkness around me. I am not separate from the world as I had separated myself from my passengers in coming here. I am connected to everything, and everything is connected to me. I breathe in. I breathe out. I am here to be connected to Africa and in doing so can connect others to Africa.

I open my eyes as the crunch of rock underfoot reaches my ears. Out beyond the light, something is coming to the water hole. From the heavy sound of it, I believe it must be several wildebeest or zebra. I peer into the darkness beyond the light. I cannot see what is coming but it is coming directly toward me rather than to the water hole itself. I squint my eyes and lean forward as if willing the animals to appear.

When it first strides from the darkness into the light, it is as if in slow-motion. There is something dreamlike about it as it materializes out of the darkness. The hair stands up on my arms and on the back of my neck as the ghostly apparition appears. Out of the darkness and into the light comes a huge, ancient bull elephant, its limestone-white skin giving him a phantasmagorical illumination. An electricity courses through me as it feels like he is my other-worldly familiar here to convey some unearthly, or earthly, message. It is the coolest effect my senses have ever had the pleasure of having to make sense of. He strides full into the light to reveal just how huge and ancient he is and a tear involuntarily leaps to my eye. It seems every time I have a dark moment of the soul, an *elephant* is there to pull me out and away from it.

I then become aware of the tromping of feet on the wood of the boardwalk and voices behind me. I peer back over my shoulder at the boardwalk and see the Finnish couple Thor and Thea almost at the gazebo. They have been my shadows on this whole trip, wanting to learn about absolutely everything along the way. No matter what rock I turned over or what tree branch I pointed at, they were there to find out about whatever it was we were encountering. If there were anyone on this trip that I would want to share this with, it would be them, especially since they, too, suffered today.

I look at the elephant now thirty yards away and closing. I look back at them also thirty yards from me. From where they are, if they run, they can cut over to me on this side of the gazebo without the elephant seeing them. If he's coming close by, I want them to see this.

"Sssst!" I hiss to them. They stop on the boardwalk and look at me. With a rapid hand wave I gesture for them to come and quickly. They get the point. They duck under the boardwalk railing and bolt over to me through the knee-high grass. I look back at the huge old bull. He is coming straight for me. I look back at them, and I smile. They have no idea what massive privilege they are about to experience.

They round the gazebo and stop to look at me. I jerk my hand at them. "Come!" They step around the gazebo and over to the pillar. The bull is no more than fifteen yards out and still coming. Thea turns to run, a look of fear on her face. I grab her arm and whisper. "It's okay, we have the electric fence right here. He won't hurt us." The fear fades to trust, and she stands still. The bull is almost to us.

At ten yards from us, he stops. He turns slightly to his right and walks forward until he is almost directly in front of us. It is almost comical how much it looks like he is modeling just for us. Once again, as on so many previous occasions when elephants have gifted me with their quiet proximity, I am filled with elation. I look at Thor and Thea on either side of me and we smile hugely at each other. We all know this is something we will never forget. *Ever.*

None of us move for over five minutes. The bull even rests his trunk on the ground as many elephants do when they are taking a nap. We sit and soak in his presence, forgetting about all other things. Finally, as if awakened from a reverie, the old bull swings his trunk in a low arc, flips it up to gives us a smell, and then moves over thirty yards to the reeds. Once there, he begins picking huge swaths of grass and stuffs them into his mouth.

I get down from the pillar. I can barely stand as the blood runs back into my legs and feet. I put a finger in front of my lips and gesture for them to follow me. I wait for the bull to put his trunk in the grass and begin collecting and then slink forward. The Finns follow my lead. We go from pillar to pillar to pillar toward the bull. As his back is to us, he cannot see us, and with all his swishing and munching, shows no sign of hearing us. We stop at the fourth pillar, again no more than fifteen yards from him. We stand there watching him feed his face for a full fifteen minutes before he decides to dematerialize into the reeds like a scene from the *Field of Dreams.*

We give each other high fives. None of us can stop smiling. I am so pleased that they got to experience this with me I can't even say anything to them. It was pure justice for a day where they had to literally leave their seats and stand in the truck's aisle next to me to listen when I was sharing knowledge about Etosha's denizens.

With this elephant, the day's woes are swept away, I am filled with the reason and joy that makes me want to be a safari guide in Africa. As we head back to the campsite, we meet another group coming noisily down the boardwalk. It occurs to me that the elephant heard them long before we did and left us as a result of their noisy presence.

"See anything?" they ask. Thor, Thea, and I look at each other and back at them. "No. Nothing." We say simultaneously. We understand how special this was, and do not want to share it. We walk back to the campsite with smiles on our faces, without a word between us and without a backward glance.

CHASING ELEPHANTS AT MIDNIGHT

"If you come across an elephant out there, Mat, you make sure to get something big between you and it like a tree, a boulder, or whatever you can. Do *not* shine your torch on it. Do *not* try and take a photo of it, and do *not* run from it. Of course, everybody knows not to run," Phillip, my South African overland guide, says to me as I head out at 8:30 p.m. into the dried riverbed that runs next to the encampment at Twyflefontein, Namibia.

"Of course," I say as if he were telling me my name is Mat. "I don't want to die."

I switch on my new flashlight, which I purchased especially for going out at night on this twenty-one day trip from Cape Town, South Africa, to Livingstone, Zambia, and Victoria Falls. Phillip frowns at me and my flashlight as if we were standing in the locker room and comparing "flashlights."

"I'll let you use mine," he says with authority. "It's much bigger." He walks over to the truck and pulls out a flashlight big enough to club an elephant to death. I immediately have flashlight envy. "Have fun," he says, handing it to me.

Phillip is a couple years older than I am, six-two, two hundred thirty pounds, and the first *safari guide* I have ever met. I liked him since the first moment I met him when I walked into a Cape Town lodge for our predeparture meeting a week and a half earlier and thought I had made a terrible mistake. I had entered the lodge, and to my left were eleven people around a table chattering away in German and no one else. I thought for certain I had the wrong lodge and the wrong group. I had chosen a company called Out of Africa Safaris from my *Coast-to-Coast* pocket guide out of all the other possible companies only because I had loved Isak Denisen's book with the same title—probably not the best way to choose a safari company I started thinking.

I searched the lodge and found Phillip in the kitchen. I asked him "Heh, is there an English-speaking group hiding here somewhere?"

Phillip laughed and offered his hand. With a big smile on his face he said in his deep voice, "You must be Mat, the *American*! Ha ha! It's you and eleven Germans! Welcome! Did you know this was a company for Germans, run by Germans?"

It turned out that Phillip's specialty is birds, which he teaches at the Nature College in South Africa. He is ranked number 142 in Southern Africa for most birds seen. I didn't know they had rankings for such a thing, but I wasn't going to argue with him. I have a great respect for Phillip already not only for his awesome bird knowledge, but also for an incredible knowledge of Africa and nature in general. There is nothing the man can't do, from cooking gourmet meals over a fire to fixing a broken truck. I do not want to disappoint him by getting myself killed in the middle of the Namibian desert.

I leave Phillip and head out from the comforting lights of Twyfelfontein's campsite toward the one-hundred-yard-wide riverbed that runs north-south. Twyfelfontein, where we have spent the day, is renowned for two things: over 2,500, 6,000-year-old rock engravings and cave paintings that has given it UNESCO World Heritage status, and the desert elephants that live in the stark dryness of Namibia's northwest. *The cave paintings were awesome, but now I want to see some desert elephants*, I think to myself as I turn south from the campsite. I switch on the mammoth flashlight. It startles me with its brilliance in the darkness of the riverbed. If I pointed it toward the sky I'm pretty sure I could blind someone on Mars with it, not that I'm complaining. I am certainly going to be able to see an elephant from a safe distance with this thing, not to mention all the other nocturnal creatures that haunt Twyfelfontein at night.

I walk along the riverbed, my feet sinking into the soft sand. It is a beautiful evening. Like in all of Namibia, the sky is filled with a million-zillion stars from horizon to horizon. We could not be more removed from civilization, and the skies tell that perfectly. I breathe in deeply and relish the clean, cool air of the desert's winter. I can't understand why everyone isn't wanting to be out here with me at night in Africa's wilds. A warmth of privilege flows through me as I scan the huge acacia's that line the riverbed. *I cannot believe I am in the middle of Namibia looking for wild African elephants in the dark!*

For my first hour I am content walking the riverbed and casting the flashlight to and fro looking for the glow of eyes, for an elephant, or whatever may be lurking in the dark of this night. I lift an occasional rock here and there hoping to find a scorpion or two or perhaps a hibernating snake. As much as I enjoy finding these critters, my quota is filled for the moment with these creatures. I do manage to find two different species of scorpion and an assortment or other insects, but my true quarry, I feel, is out there somewhere. I'm pretty sure desert elephants are not going to be found under rocks.

I turn back north and hike past the firelights in the campsite. I realize, seeing it from an elephant's eye view, that if there are elephants in the riverbed, there can certainly be elephants in the campsite. There are no fences to keep them out. After about five hundred yards, a curve in the riverbed heads east. Another three hundred yards from there, I arrive at a circular, concrete cistern. It is six and a half feet high and fifteen feet in diameter. It is filled with water. I reason it must be a holder for the camp's water or a well of some sort. I continue past the cistern. At about seventy yards east from it, a small canyon leads north away from the riverbed. I stand at the mouth of it and look at the canyon walls. They increase in height the farther one enters into it. It is darker in the canyon and inviting for adventure.

As I have the ultimate dark destroyer in my hands, I feel I can conquer it. My common sense, for once this night, gets the better of me. *If you go in there, and it has a dead end, and an elephant comes in behind you. You're going to be turned into grape jelly.* I decide not to go in. *What now?* I don't want to go back but it is pushing two and half hours already, and if I haven't seen an elephant yet I doubt I will. *Maybe the elephants are too afraid of the campsite and stay away from it,* I reason. I decide to head back toward the camp. I am more than a little discouraged and my arm hurts from carrying the monstrous flashlight.

When I arrive back at our campsite's fire only Anz, twenty-three, one of my two tent mates is up and present. He smokes a cigarette with his hand stuck in the thick shock of hair that usually sticks straight up from his head. Anz and Nora, a lovely 22 year old and our other tent mate (after Phillip's snoring drove her into our tent), work quite hard on the trip cooking, cleaning, and packing the truck as Phillip's interns. They are usually the only ones at the fire at night relaxing after long days. I always invite them to come with me on my night excursions (as I do everyone) but they are usually too tired to come. (Nora, to her credit, once came out with me one night at our Fish River Canyon campsite, but was only mildly impressed when the only creature we found was a massive armored ground cricket, which looked like something straight out of *Starship Troopers*.)

Anz looks exhausted. He does, however, manage to make exhaustion look cool like most things he does. I can't help but think that he should have his own TV show like *German Rebel Without a Cause*.

"Find anything?" he asks as I appear in the light of the fire.

"Just a couple critters," I say dejectedly. "Where is Nora?" I ask. He jabs a thumb toward our tent.

"She vas tired," he says as if speaking about himself.

"No elephants?" he asks.

"Not a one," I say and plop down on a stool near the fire.

"An elephant I vould like to see as vell," he says.

I can't tell if he is telling the truth because I know he finds me an oddity not only because I am the only non-German on an overland truck with a company that does trips exclusively for Germans, but also because I insist on spending a great deal of my evenings out looking for God-knows-what in the wilds of everywhere we go. His amusement notwithstanding, I take it as an invitation, although it was just probably a factual statement. "You want to go back out there and look?" I offer excitedly.

He considers it in his cool way and says, "Vy not?" He flicks his cigarette into the fire.

"Do you think Nora wants to come?" I ask.

"Nah! She's asleep. Come, vee go!"

I lead him back toward the riverbed. I tell him the rules that Phillip imparted to me. He nods in his cool way. He's not a fool. He'll find something to put between him and the elephant. *Me*, if necessary I'm quite certain. I turn on Phillip's flashlight and give Anz my flashlight as mine is significantly better than his. We head south once again toward the rock pile I encountered earlier.

Halfway there, a tall, feline form races from a fallen tree in the middle of the riverbed. In a flash of spots, ears, and tail it bolts across the sand and then disappears in the thick bush lining the riverbed.

Although it was the size of a lynx with a longer tail we are certain it is a small leopard. I have yet to learn that there is such a creature known as a serval, which it actually is. We search the ground at the spot where it entered the bush for spoor. Sure enough, the spoor is crystal clear in the sand leading from the riverbed.

"Let's track it," I offer. Anz scrunches up his face and shakes his head.

"No. Vat if dere is an elephant?"

"That's why we're here right? C'mon! Look at this flashlight. We're not going to miss an elephant," I say.

"You can go," he says nonchalantly.

I shrug and regard the darkness beyond the riverbed. *It would be awesome to find the cat sitting on an elephant*, I think. With this thought in mind I leave Anz and enter the trees.

I follow the cat prints as far as they go. They disappear in a maze of small bushes, grasses, and rocks. I shine the light in every direction but see nothing. It will have to be enough that we at least got to see a flash of a creature neither of us had ever seen before in our lives. I return to the riverbed where Anz smokes, leaning against the fallen tree the cat had been occupying.

I decide to eschew heckling him about his smoking and how it is not beneficial for finding elephants. I begin inspecting the nooks and crannies of the tree around him. I peel back the bark and shine the light under it.

"For vat are you looking?" Anz asks. "Anything, really," I respond. "Fallen, dead trees like this are a great place to find scorpions." I can't help but smile when Anz launches himself from the trunk swearing in German. "Don't worry. They are more afraid of you then you are them." He isn't convinced. I shine the light on the ground at our feet and see another creature of interest. Anz is going to *love* this.

I stoop to the ground and point at the upside-down conical holes in the sand. "Here's a really cool creature," I say. Anz stoops his tall frame over and peers at the holes. "These are called ant lions." (I would come to learn they are one of the "Little Five.") They build these holes in the soft substrate and wait for ants or other small insects to fall in. They can also flick sand at potential prey near the brim. They knock them into the bottom where they wait to grab them in their huge mandibles and then suck the juices from them. Cool, huh?" He shakes his head at me again. I'm pretty sure if he ever met an ant lion he'd find some room for it on the bottom of his boot.

I stand up from the ant lion holes and fumble the flashlight. I grab it before it hits the ground. I follow the light beam to the sand and what it illuminates there. It takes me a moment to realize at what I'm looking. "*Holy sh-t*!" I exclaim, a bolt of excitement shooting through me.

"Vat?" Anz says.

I point at the ground and the enormous, one-and-a-half-foot, ovular print in the sand at our feet. "Vas is dis?" he asks my beaming face.

My very first elephant footprint! I can barely contain my excitement. I want to jump up and down and celebrate with whoops and calls, but I don't want to scare away the elephant that made these prints, if he is nearby. "That, my German friend, is an elephant footprint."

As cool as he is, even Anz is excited at this. "Dat's cool," he says.

"Let's follow them," I suggest. He nods his head in acquiescence.

Like two bloodhounds we follow the huge footprints. I can hear the blood rushing in my head as my adrenalized heart pounds in my chest. We shine our lights crazily in every direction. Every twenty steps or so we stop and listen to hear if there are breaking of branches. We know we won't hear the elephant's own steps. Phillip already told us his story about how elephants make no noise when they walk:

"I was in the Delta with a buddy camping. We were supposed to take turns watching the fire, you know, to make sure nothing grabbed us in the middle of the night. Just to make sure, we always sleep with our heads closer to the fire rather than our feet so if any hyena or lions are brave enough to come close, they will grab our feet first and not our heads. Anyway, it was my buddy's turn to watch the fire in the early hours of the morning so after waking him, I went to sleep.

"Well, I wake up with the sun already up and look around. The fire is nothing but ashes. My buddy is asleep on the other side of the fire, snoring away. I'm pissed so I stand up to throw water on him and tear him a new one. As I stand up and look around, I'm shocked by what I see. Everywhere in the campsite are elephant footprints. I look down at my bed roll and get that feeling, you know, that terrible but relieved feeling you get when you've just survived something that you're pretty sure should have killed you. Well, *there are elephant footprints on one side of where I was laying and elephant footprints on the other side of where I was laying.* Same with my buddy. A herd of elephants not only walked through our campsite without us hearing them, but they *walked right over us* without us even hearing them."

Anz and I follow the spoor to the side of the riverbed no more than two hundred yards from the campsite. There is a huge imprint in the bank, which shows that the elephant had been rolling in the sand and against the roots there. It looks like it was made a few minutes before. It is one big mother of an imprint. The footprints, however, end here.

The elephant obviously left the riverbed at this point and went into the trees. Greatly impressed with the size of the imprint I consider my options. Following this gargantuan creature into the trees seems a little less inviting than it did before. I do climb the bank to shine the flashlight into the depths of the bush. My probing light illuminates nothing but the trees blowing in the gentle wind. I listen but only get the quiet whisper of the wind through the leaves. I frown. I realize I am not going to see an elephant in the true wilds of Africa with no fences, no protection, an elephant utterly free of the confines of human influence.

I climb down to Anz. He shrugs his shoulders. He won't show it with his coolness, but it is obvious he is disappointed as well. We walk back to the campsite in silence even as I continue to shine the light in every direction just in case our elephant is watching us from the other side of the riverbed. We reach the road that leads to the campsite still another fifty yards away from us. I stop as Anz continues toward the lights of the campsite. I am overcome by an overwhelming feeling that I am going to miss something great if I go back to the campsite now.

Anz stops and looks back at me. "Vat are you doing?" he asks.

"I gotta see an elephant," I say from my rooted spot. "This is my only chance on foot to see an elephant in the true wilds of Africa. I'm going to stay out a little longer." He nods at me, understanding.

"Tanks for the walk," he says and walks toward the campsite.

I feel a little foolish standing there with the flashlight. There is a million, zillion square miles of desert around Twyfelfontein. I look back at where we had come from. I have no idea when those tracks were made. Even if I keep guard all night in the riverbed, the odds of seeing an elephant are slim to none. I turn to look back at Anz. He is just about at the small reception area when I hear, *Crrrraaaaaacccckkkkk!*

I spin around and shine my light in the direction of the noise. A hundred yards away on the other side of the riverbed, the bushes and trees shake like a scene from *King Kong*. A huge bull elephant breaks through the bush and strides proudly into the riverbed. I can't believe it. My mouth drops open mouthing the word *ELEPHANT,* but nothing comes out. I turn to Anz's departing form and, like a scene in a comedy routine, start jumping up and down and pointing. "*ELEPHANT! ELEPHANT!*" I hiss at him.

Anz doesn't hear me. He is just past the reception building. I want him to see this, but I don't want to scream as it might scare the elephant. I also don't want to miss the elephant, if I run back to Anz. I look back toward the elephant. He heads north, obviously on a mission. I turn back toward Anz. I look back toward the elephant. All I need to do is sprint to the huge tree in the middle of the riverbed and that would separate me from the elephant by only forty yards. I turn back to Anz. I can't let him *not* see this elephant. I make my decision. I run back toward Anz, leaping up in the air every fifth step, hissing as loudly as I can. "*Elephant, Anz! Elephant!*"

Anz stops as my hissing reaches him. I race up to him completely maniacal. "Come on! Come on! Elephant!" His eyes gleam, and he bunches his fists in front of him. "Do you have a camera?" I ask desperately.

He scrunches his eyes at me. "*Vat do you need a camera for?*"

"Mine broke at Sossusvlei 'cuz of the sand. Get your camera and meet me by that huge tree in the riverbed! I'll keep an eye on him!" I say. He considers me as one would a total nut. "Go!" I push him. He races back to the tents. I race back to the riverbed.

The bull feeds off a tree fifty yards on the other side of the tree, which stands smack in the middle of the riverbed. I run to the tree using it to block his line of vision and mine. Every ten steps I lean off to a side to check on him. It looks like I'm storming a bunker. I get to the tree and can barely contain myself. *A true wild elephant in the completely unfettered wilds of Africa!*

I can't help myself and point the flashlight on him. He turns when the light hits his eyes. Phillip's words find their way back into my head. *Don't shine your light on the elephant.* "Just on his butt," I whisper to myself as I shine the light on his huge wrinkled caboose. I am giddy to the point of stupidity when Anz arrives with his camera dangling from his hand.

He ducks down behind the exposed roots of the tree with me. Now we both look like we are storming a bunker. We both slowly slide up and peer over at the elephant as he munches on the tree. Suddenly, I am consumed with what may very well be the greatest compulsion and idiotic idea I have ever had in my whole life. *I NEED a photo of this elephant. I need proof that I was in the wilds of Africa with a wild elephant with nothing between us but wildness.*

"Give me the camera," I say deadly serious.

"Vy?" Anz asks. "What do you mean 'Vy'? I'm going to get a photo of the elephant," I say.

"My camera won't take a photo from this far in the dark," he says.

"Duh," I respond. "That's why we're going to follow him keeping these trees between us and him." I point at the trees that line the middle of the riverbed. "We just follow the trees and then if he gets far from the bank, we use the bank for cover."

Anz blinks at me trying to understand just how crazy I might actually be. "Ve've seen de elephant. Vy don't ve just keep it in our mind as a great memory."

I am too far gone to listen. "No, that's bullsh-t. We need a photo," I say like an army captain convincing his men to storm the machinegun nest.

"You're f—king crazy," Anz says, but I'm not listening. I look at him intensely. He shakes his head and hands me the camera.

The bull meanders north, parallel to the riverbed, stopping to sample some of the endless delicacies around him. I wait for him to stop fifty meters farther down. "Come on. We're going to that tree." I point to another huge tree with a mass of branches and grasses around its base, halfway between us and the elephant. I crouch down and race for the tree, trying to hold a line where I keep the tree between us and the elephant's line of sight. I get to the tree and am happy to see Anz right behind me. I offer the flashlight to Anz. Going against Phillip's exact advice I say, "Point it at the elephant but not in his eyes."

Anz takes it from me. "You're f—king crazy," he repeats.

"I got that memo," I retort.

I climb up on one of the huge roots where I have a perfect view of the elephant. Anz points the torch right at the elephant's backside. I hit the zoom on the camera and get the elephant on the screen. It isn't great but an elephant can at least be recognized. I push the button. The flash shines out across the distance between us. The elephant turns toward us and I snap another photo. Anz drops the light from the elephant. "Wait! One more!" I hiss back at him. He has ducked back down behind the roots of the tree. I look back at the elephant. Obviously perturbed by the flash, the bull heads north. I look down at the camera to see if the photo took so we can leave the bull alone. There is nothing on the camera but darkness. "Sh-t," I mutter aloud.

"Let's go! You got your photo," Anz hisses, his eyes peeking over the roots.

"Nope." I raise the camera up as if he could see something. "We gotta follow him. It didn't take." He groans.

"You are the craziest f—king American I ever met!" he yells at me.

"Great. Come on," I say.

I jog in a crouched position after the disappearing elephant. He is following the riverbed at about ten yards from the bank in the trees. The trees mostly obscure him, but there are spaces farther down on the bank where I can take the photo. There are, however, no trees to cover Anz. As I reach another tree in the riverbed, I stop. I don't want Anz to get any closer, even though he has the flashlight. As obsessed as I am, I don't want to get another person killed because of a photo. Myself, okay. Someone else, definitely not. I wave at him to stop where he is. He stops and crouches behind another smaller tree. There is no way he is going to miss the elephant killing me.

I beeline for the spot thirty yards down away, using the bank of the river as a shield. I stop at a point where the bank is four feet tall. I am twenty yards from where the riverbed takes its ninety-degree angle east from us. If the elephant keeps his course, he will go through an open spot in the vegetation. Then, I can jump up, snap a photo, and then hide down again in the riverbed. If I miss, he may cross the riverbed north of us where I can get another chance to get him. I doubt the animal is going to come looking for me. I hit the spot and listen for the elephant.

I can hear the branches being pushed aside by his bulk and try to measure the noise in relation to my position. I don't want to jump up and the elephant be right there. I'm sure an elephant can climb down four feet. It sounds like he's going away from me. I jump up and see his enormous butt heading directly away from me, already fifteen yards away. To Anz's credit he has the pachyderm in the beam of the flashlight from his position.

I hold the camera up and hit the button again and again. The only thing the flash illuminates is his enormous butt disappearing into the bush. A butt is good enough for me. I check the camera. Nothing. It has focused on the trees that were directly in front of me, and the rest is darkness. It is like I was taking photos of a phantom.

Anz appears at my shoulder. "Did you get your photo?" he asks, breathless.

I frown and show him the camera. *Nicht*.

"C'mon. Let's go back. You're not gonna get a photo," he begs.

"Yes, we are," I insist. He can see by the grim determination in my eyes, I will get myself killed in order to have this photo. "A wild elephant, in the wilds of Africa. I'm going to get this photo," I say.

He shakes his head. Somehow he has fallen for my insanity and made this moronic endeavor his own.

We slink down to where the bank curves east. We peer around the bushes to see if the elephant is crossing the riverbank. There is nothing there, and we can't hear anything. It is as if the animal has disappeared. I nearly pop my eyes out of their sockets trying to penetrate the bush on both sides of the river. "He must be in the trees on our side of the river," I whisper.

I judge the distance across to the other side. There are no trees to hide in this part of the riverbed. If I am going to cross the riverbed to see the elephant back on the other side, then I am going to have to fly. If the elephant is in the trees just east of where we are and I startle it, it is going to chase me down and turn me into jelly. I make the decision. "I am going across." I don't wait for Anz to answer. I bolt for it.

I am halfway across when I realize just how moronic this effort is. The elephant could be five yards east of where we were sitting near the riverbank. It could come right after me. I know elephants are faster than humans. I put the burner on and turbo my way the hundred yards across. It is the longest hundred yards I've ever done in the shortest time. If I were in the Olympics, I'd be taking home the gold. Not a second after I hit the opposite bank, Anz lands right behind me.

"Dat was fast," he says.

No scheisse.

We squat down behind the roots of another tree and look back at the side from which we have come. All along that side of the bank, there is nothing as far east as we can see. The bull has disappeared. A stab of disappointment hits me. It's like I am six again and miss catching a lizard. "Maybe if we go up farther on this side, we'll see him," I say.

Anz and I both stand up and he yells, "Dere he is!"

Seventy-five yards in front of us, the bull crosses the river-bed. He is heading directly toward the cistern. The light goes off in my head. *Water cistern. Elephant. Elephant, water cistern. The cistern is for the desert elephants! Duh.* Another light goes off. *All I had to do was sit next to the cistern and eventually the elephants would have come to me!*

"Come on!" I hiss to Anz. He doesn't bother to protest. He follows on my heels from the safety of the bank to another tree fifty yards from the cistern. We duck behind the tree as the elephant comes up from the riverbed. He beelines for the cistern. "*Yes!*" escapes my lips.

The cistern is completely out in the open. The only thing between our tree and the cistern is a sapling as thick as my finger and five feet high. It looks like a pom-pom stuck on a pointer stick. It is no more than twenty-five yards from where the elephant splashes noisily in the cistern. That tree is categorically *not* what Phillip had in mind when he told me to have a tree between me and an elephant. I have already broken every one of his rules and probably a whole bunch of a lot of other people's rules so what is one more? I make the decision.

"Shine the light on the elephant," I instruct Anz.

"My camera can't reach it from here," he says.

"I know." I hand him my flashlight as well. "Just keep them on the elephant." Before he can protest, I sprint for the sapling. As I bolt in a crouch I think I hear Anz blurt, "But my camera…"

Fortunately, the elephant is busy splashing himself with the cool waters of the cistern as I make it to the sapling. I immediately turn sideways as if I am hiding behind a wall. It is the most ridiculous thing I have ever done in my life. The adrenaline in my system is nearly uncontrollable. My hands are shaking. I look back at Anz. To his credit or discredit, he shines the lights on the elephant. I look back to the thirsty pachyderm and see that with the light on the elephant and it being in the open in the moonlight, I have a perfect photo.

I focus once again on the bull. I wait for him to splash water on himself to disguise the flash. He does, and I snap the photo. It doesn't work. The bull stops his splashing and listens. I stand perfectly still "behind" the sapling. The elephant would be laughing if he looked in my direction. Instead, he turns away from the cistern and heads east, toward the canyon. "No," I say out loud as if trying to keep him from leaving. I know if he goes into the canyon I won't be able to go in after him. There is only one thing I can do. Crouched like a predator, I sprint for the cistern, using it to keep me from the elephant's line of sight.

As I make the cistern I almost crush my skull against it. Stopping from a running crouch is not nearly as easy as one would think and harder still jacked up on adrenaline. I press myself against the cool concrete and steel myself. My heart feels like it's about to explode from my chest. *Just jump up and take the photo, Mat.* I take a deep breath and I jump straight up with the camera held above me ready to fire. I'm expecting to see a departing elephant butt just beyond the cistern. What I get instead is *a* giant *elephant head* not five yards from the other side of the cistern, his ears wide open. My eyes almost pop out of my skull. *He stopped and came back!*

Without thinking, my finger hits the take button and the flash bursts from the camera. I duck and listen. I count, "One-one-thousand" and push the camera up above me. *Click!* I jerk back down. I count, "One-one-thousand" once again. I shove the camera back above me. *Click!* I pull it back down. I listen. I hear nothing.

It only then occurs to me that if the rest of the night's activities didn't win me Biggest Moron in the World Award already, I am definitely winning it for this. It would be easy for the elephant to stomp his way *right through* the cistern and crush me. If he decided to come around either side, my only option would be to try and run around the cistern until he got tired of chasing me or he caught me and turned me into mashed potato. *I am the epitome of vulnerable and for what? A photo. That's going to look great on my gravestone.*

I consider my options and realize quite quickly I have only one. I need to make a break for it. I may startle him by racing out from behind the cistern. That will give me the drop on him and allow at least ten to fifteen extra yards for me to get behind the tree fifty yards away. I gather my feet beneath me and listen. One...two...*three!* I bolt for the tree and Anz.

I feel like I am flying over the ground as my legs pump beneath me like two angry pistons in overdrive. Having never run for my life before, I'm finding the experience rather exhilarating. Anz's white face is indistinguishable as I rapidly approach the tree, but I picture it as a mask of horror and disbelief. At twenty-five yards the exhilaration morphs into a sickening horror as I trip. I go from vertical, rocketing to horizontal flight. I half expect the elephant to pluck me from the air and crush me in his trunk. I hold my hand with Anz's camera high above my head, as my body descends toward the ground. I go down hard, my body splayed like Superman. I bounce several times and then curl. I immediately roll to my feet, the camera unharmed. Me, not so much.

I look behind me ready to see the elephant's huge bulk about to crush me into oblivion. Instead, there is nothing. I slow to a stop and search the distance for the animal. The elephant is already seventy yards away and almost at the canyon. I bend over and dust off my slightly torn knees. Anz comes running up to me. "My camera!" I can't say I blame him for caring more about it than me. I hand it to him for inspection. "Check the photos," I say breathlessly. He looks at me with utter disbelief and shakes his head.

"You crazy f—king American!" he says and checks his camera.

I check myself for broken bones while Anz makes sure I didn't kill his camera during my momentary lapses of reason. A look of relief passes over his face as he sees his camera is fine. He then calls up the photos and flips through them, one eyebrow up, strategically expressing his disdain. I figure after all that I've just put him through, he deserves at least to see them first, although I'm obviously dying to see them. "Nice ones," he says and hands me the camera.

I flip one and then another. I flip again and again with that terrible sense of despair one has when one believes one has braved death to succeed and learns that one has failed after all. Every photo is of the opposite side of the cistern. *Someone* didn't quite have the proper angle to get the elephant. I hang my head. "I can't believe it," I say dejectedly.

Anz lets it sink in for a moment. He then hits me on the shoulder. "Heh. No one can tell you, you didn't try."

I laugh and hand him back his camera. "You think?" I say.

Back at the campsite, Anz and I plop onto our stools by the fire. I can barely stand my own smell as I peel my adrenaline-soaked shirt from my pits. Chasing elephants at midnight is sweaty, exhausting business. I smile as I peer into the fire. I know that even if I didn't get the photos, I am as thrilled as I have ever been in my life. *I got up close and personal with a desert elephant in the middle of Namibia's wilds! What else do I need to experience in this lifetime?* I look over at Anz.

He lights up a cigarette, pushes his mop of hair away from his face, and shakes his head at me. "You are one crazy American."

I laugh again. I have a feeling he's going to remember this night just as long as I will. "Do me a favor, my man," I say with a huge grin.

"Vat?" Anz asks.

"Don't tell Phillip about this."

CHAPTER TWO

TRIALS AND TRIBULATIONS

AND THE DARWIN AWARD GOES TO...

GWYNN

Gwynn, with her pretty, lightly freckled Irish face shrouded in flaming red hair looks at me deathly serious, "Ahm not gooin' to the Sahrengeti and stayin' in a cahmpsite without a fence aroun' it. Furget it. Ahm *not* gooin'."

I smile at her. Many people come to Africa believing it is an assurety that they are going to be eaten by lions or hyenas if they camp in its wilds. No fence around the campsite in the middle of Serengeti sounds like a bad idea to just about everybody except those of us who have done it, survived it, and are thrilled by the idea of doing it again. Obviously, the animals can't come right up to your tent if you're stuck behind a fence.

"You cannot miss the Serengeti, Gwynn. It is arguably the most amazing place on Earth. To miss it, is to miss East Africa. Besides, do you think I'd let you get eaten? It's bad for business." She's not impressed with my joke even though I am getting to her.

"How'll you protect meh? Are you gooin' to wrastle a lion to the groun' if it attahcks meh?" I nod at her. "Exactly. Happens all the time. In fact, I've wrestled so many lions to the ground that they've stopped coming to the campsite." A smile tugs at the corner of her face. "All right. I'll coom. On *one* condishun." She taps her finger on the air between us. "Ahm stayin' in *yer* tent with *you*." I chuckle at that. It is not lost on me that having a lovely lady staying in my tent may look a little odd to the rest of the passengers, but I'm willing to take one for the team if it means she gets to come. I can't stand the idea of my people missing the Serengeti and Ngorongoro Crater. It is like missing days in Heaven while you're still alive.

When we arrive at our campsite in the Seronera area, Gwynn gazes around to confirm the fact that there are no fences. I can tell she's thinking that perhaps they had built a fence since the last time I was there a month previously. The truth is, not only does it not have a fence around it, but on one occasion, lions killed a buffalo in the *middle* of the campsite, and no one could exit their tents for an entire morning until the pride had finished eating and sauntered off.

I ask Gwynn how close to the toilets does she want to be. She marches me, with the tent bag on my shoulder, to a point right next to the toilet block. To her credit, she helps me put the tent up even as her eyes dart into the semidarkness of the acacia woods stretching out around us. "Are we close enough to the toilets for you?" I ask. We are actually as close to the toilets as we could possibly be without actually being *in* the toilets.

"Aye. It's foine. It doesn't really mahtter, right, anyweh? Yer gooin' to get up with me fer the toilets in the middle of the night if I haff to go, right?"

"Yes, Gwynn. I will be going to the toilets with you in the middle of the night as I promised." She nods at me, her eyes casting furtively about.

At dinner I reiterate the process necessary for getting out of one's tent in the middle of the night in Africa's wilds. "First, you listen. If you don't hear anything, you may unzip the tent and shine your light in the darkness to see if there are any eyes shining back. If there are eyes, you stay in the tent. If not, you may stand up and shine the light 360 degrees around and behind the tent to see if there is anything shining back. If not, you may climb out and do your business. If you run into anything on your way to the toilets, do not run. Stay still, make yourself really big, and scream. I will then come running to see what has found you. Does everyone understand?" I look at everyone's eyes to see if all have gotten the memo. Gwynn stares absently into the fire but I don't say anything to her about her apparent disinterest. After all, I will be in fairly close proximity to her if anything goes wrong.

It is around 2:00 a.m. when Gwynn whispers in the darkness. "I haff to go." I wake up instantly. I never sleep deeply when out in the wilds of Africa, in case I need to fulfill my promise of assisting someone with an animal problem or an animal with a people problem. "Okay." I sit up and fumble for my light.

"Do you want me to go with you?" I ask.

"No, no. Ahm foine." She wraps her jacket around her shoulders and bends to obtain what I assume is her light.

She searches the wall of the tent instead. After what I've told her and the other passengers, I'm certain she isn't looking for the zipper. She can't seem to locate what she's looking for. She stops. *Click*! Her light flicks on. It not only illuminates the tent, but also the fact that she is not wearing a whole lot more than her jacket. I try not to stare at her underwear staring me in the face. "Ah, here tis," she says triumphantly. She unzips the tent with a flourish and moves to step out. I am flabbergasted.

"What are you doing?" I hiss. I attempt to grab her jacket. I get her underwear instead.

"Heh! Whaddya dooin'?" she objects as I pull her back into the tent.

"What am *I* doing?" I ask, unhooking my fingers from her undies elastic. "What are *you* doing? Didn't you hear a thing I told you at dinner? You can't just get out of the tent. You didn't even listen to hear if there was anything out there!"

She blinks at me. "Well, I mean, *yer here*. Why do I haff to do all that uther stoof?"

I laugh at that. "It isn't going to do you a lot of good if I'm in here and you step out there and there is a lion or hyena sitting there." She looks at me like I hurt her feelings or maybe just because I stretched her undies a bit. I soften considerably to accommodate her wounded pride. "Hold on. Let me take a look."

I listen and hear nothing except the buzz sawing of someone snoring. I shine my light into the campsite but see only the humps of the other tents. I stand up with my feet still inside the tent and shine my light around left and right. I spin around and shine the light back behind the tent. I stop, my blood turning to ice. I shake my head thinking of what may have been possible if Gwynn had stepped out here without looking. Gwynn senses my hesitation and stands up next to me.

"Wa tis it?" she asks. I point back behind the tent and her hands claw into my arm. "Ohhhh!" she squeals. *Five hyena* stand not twenty feet from the back of the tent, their ten eyes shining like fiery, red coals back at us. I shake my head and extricate my wounded arm from her clutch.

"Yeah. That's why I want you to do all those things I told you before you get out of the tent."

I snarl at them and hiss. I wave my arms and smack the tent. They retreat ten yards with a couple of hoots but stop and look back at us. I hiss and snarl again at them, occasionally smacking the tent until they retreat into the trees, a good fifty yards out. "Do you want to use the toilet?" I ask her.

"No! Ah'll pee here next to the tent," she says sheepishly.

"I'll be in here," I say ducking back into the tent.

"No!" She grabs my arm again. "You stay doon on *thaht* side of the tent and Ah'll pee on this one. Cover yer ears and hum so you cahn't hear me peein'."

I snicker and step out of the tent with my light in the hyenas' eyes. I move to my side of the tent and hunker down choosing the *StarWars* theme to ensure maximum sound blockage. She squats on the other side of the tent and does her business. After a moment or two, she grabs my arm and pulls it away from my ear. "Okay," she says. "Ah'm funished."

I smile at her but don't say anything. She climbs back into the tent. I admire the hyenas for a few moments and then clamber back into the tent after her. I can't say that they would have definitely eaten her, but she certainly wasn't helping herself *not* get eaten.

DEVON

I walk along Thebe River Camp's electric fence that leads me straight back to the campsite usually reserved for Overlanders. From there, it is easy to see the Chobe River and whatever may come down to it, particularly at night. There are no fences around Chobe National Park so the town of Kasane, which sits in the middle of it, is privileged to have any type of beastie walking its streets and yards. Thebe would be no different if it didn't have the electrified fence around its premises. It is a fence that they have to turn off when the Chobe River floods during the rainy season so as not to electrocute everyone on the premises.

As I approach our campsite, the sounds of excitement reach my ears. A group has gathered at the back fence, which I can barely see through the green seven-foot nets put up to block the campsite proper from the parking area. Off to the right and down at the river, not more than forty yards from where the group stands, is a herd of elephants thirstily drinking from the river. It is a little strange for the elephants to come down riverside this early in the afternoon. Usually the elephants won't come this close to the campsite unless it is late at night, as they don't appreciate our presence as much as we do theirs.

I jog the rest of the way to the campsite and walk around the netted area. Everyone is gathered with their cameras at ready. Some are already snapping photos, and they are not of the elephants. *Not a good sign.* Most are laughing and cheering, which makes me even more nervous to say the least. A cheering group of tourists is rarely a good thing when large African animals are concerned. I rush over to them to see what the ruckus is. When I reach them and peer over a few shoulders my head immediately goes into incredulous shaking. "*What the f…?*"

Caught within the electric wiring of the fence that harbors nine thousand volts when on is Devon. His six-six gangly frame is tied up in Gumby-like, octopoidal precision in all seven wires, like he is trying his best to ensure absolute electrocution. When people are aware of my presence they make way for me. It is quite obvious to them by the look on my face that although this situation seems funny it is categorically not funny. My passenger is trying his best to ensure his trip to Africa is his last trip ever.

Devon becomes aware of the quietness and change in the people around him. He looks back and sees me. He smiles sheepishly. "Heh, heh. Hi, Mat," he says inanely. I consider him for a moment and gather my tongue before it says something less than savory to our "campsite idiot." After all, it is Devon's first trip out of Canada, and he is barely twenty-two years old. Common sense seems the least common of the senses sometimes.

"Um, Devon. Tell me something. Does this seems like a good idea crawling through an electric fence that may not be on at the moment but could come on at any time to go see a herd of elephants that are drinking from the river? Not only are they drinking at the river with several little ones among them, but if they were to turn around and want to flee, they would be trapped between an electric fence and the river with the only thing between them being you. Do you think that would be an ideal situation for you?"

He stops struggling within the wires, and I can feel the ridiculousness coursing through him. "Um, no. Not a good idea," he says.

"I have to agree, my man," I say. "What do you think? Maybe you could crawl back through and admire the elephants from this side of the fence?" Devon nods and struggles to come back the way he came.

He finally drags himself from the clutches of the fence. He stands to his full height towering over me, with his head drooped in sufficient repentance. "You don't want your first trip out of Canada to be your last, right?"

"Right, Mat. Right."

STEF

I get done talking about the intricacies of lion prides and as I finish I hear, "Pss, pss. Pss, pss. PSSSSS! Here kitty! Here kitty, kitty!" from the back corner of the truck. My face darkens and the anger courses through me. For the past three hours I have been telling Stef not to make noises at animals when we pull alongside them here in Etosha National Park. This would be the third time and the last. I can't see her behind the last seat in the truck and assume she might even be leaning out the window. It is easy for a lion to jump up the eight feet to the window and make a welcome meal of Stef.

I look out the window at the mating lions not five yards from the side of the truck to see if Stef is disturbing them. She is. The male gets up from his position alongside his female counterpart and moves a safe distance from the truck. It makes me extremely angry. Not only is it extremely dangerous to be bothering lions when they are mating, but I also know that if people disturb these animals they will stay away from vehicles. In staying away from vehicles, they will crawl out of sight.

If people are not seeing animals in parks like Etosha, they will not come. If they aren't coming out to see these animals, there will be no reason to have them occupying space in land that can be used for other purposes across Africa. I have explained as much to Stef but she doesn't seem to quite get it.

"Stef! This is the last time I'm telling you. You do it again and you will not be coming with us to the Delta or Chobe!" The other passengers jump on board and begin castigating her. That saves me the trouble of really telling her how much I'm learning not to like her. The other passengers have already sat her down earlier in the trip and told her what they thought of her. "If you wouldn't make every conversation about you and ask us questions just so you can interrupt us and tell us endless stories about yourself, we might actually like you. Everything is always about you, and we just don't want to deal with you," they told her.

"Okay, okay. I just wanted them to look at me so I can get a good photo." She protests like a three-year-old.

"I've already explained to you about this, Stef. I won't explain it again," I say tersely. She sits back in her seat and sulks while everybody dully ignores her for what will be the rest of the day. As we pull away from the lions, I feel a bit for Stef. It is quite obvious she lacks some serious common sense and people skills. The strange truth about her is she is actually quite bright in her way and in Vancouver runs a clinic to help battered woman. I am feeling a little compassion for her until we reach the campsite.

My compassion evaporates instantaneously when Nick, the driver of our overland vehicle, walks up to me with a look of incredulity on his face. "Rafiki, how crazy is that muzungu from Canada?" he states.

"I'm sorry, Rafiki. I told her that if she makes any more noises at the animals she won't be joining the safaris."

He looks at me and laughs. "Making noises? Did you see what she was doing besides making noises?" he asks. I'm dreading his telling me. I shake my head, no. "She was leaning out the window with her sweater, shaking it and yelling, "Here kitty, kitty! Here kitty, kiiittttyyy!"

I am not surprised but at the same time flummoxed. "I guess, my man, we'll have to lock her up on any other excursions," I say. "That will be best for everyone," he says. "Especially her."

HAE SOON

"I have a headache, and my flend flom the other tluck say I have maralia so I have maralia," Hae Soon says to me without equivocation. I am nearly at my wit's end with Hae Soon. For two weeks she has been insisting that she speaks and understands English perfectly yet shows absolutely no sign of this in doing everything I have told her not to do every chance she gets.

I look at her in the dim light of the truck's inner cabin as seriously as possible. "Hae Soon. You do not have malaria. If you have a headache and your body aches, it is probably the flu that has been going through the truck that I myself had last week. If it was malaria, you would not be sitting here talking with me like you are. You have no chills, a low fever, and it is flu season here in Southern Africa. We have been in Namibia for the past two weeks where there is no malaria, and there are almost no mosquitoes this time of year. It is not impossible but extremely, extremely unlikely," I say emphatically. She looks at me with a determined look. "Maralia." *Rrrrrrrrr*.

I think back to the first time I met her at the predeparture. She sat through it in her funky green raincoat that hid her waiflike figure. Her hood and sunglasses served to cover her almost transparent whitish/olive skin. It was as if she were a rock star or a vampire trying to hide out from the world but only succeeded in drawing even more attention to herself. I later asked her why she wore this particular getup. She told me that she prized having as light-colored skin as possible and shunned the sun. After that, as soon as she would climb on the truck, she would pull her hood down over her eyes and sleep on the truck like a drugged narcoleptic. It was quite funny at times to see her as it looked like we had a stuffed raincoat sitting in the seat by itself.

When we had reached the first border I told her that that she needed to take off her raincoat and sunglasses when she went into the border crossing. So it was with more than a little disappointment that I saw her walk up to the border control still sporting her spy outfit. If they hadn't seen her South Korean passport, they might think she was a terrorist trying to hide from satellite photography. They, of course, requested her to disrobe when she reached the desk to get her passport stamped.

Later I ask her why she went up to the desk with her entire regalia on after I told her not to. She vehemently pronounced "I speak pelfect Engrish, Mat! I go to school in Phiraderphia and am concelt jazz pianist. I undelstand evelyting you say! Stop terring me I don't undelstand," she insists to me.

And so it went from there.

So having her in front of me insisting she had malaria should come as no surprise. "Listen. If you'd like, I can take you to the clinic, and we can get you checked out right now. It is eight o'clock. We can find a clinic by around ten. After that it will take at least a couple hours until they tell you the same thing I have told you. It will then take us another couple hours to get back here, or…" I take a deep breath before I begin.

"Why don't you take some ibuprofen or acetaminophen and see if that works over the next couple hours. I will check on you, and if you're not feeling better we will go to the clinic. If you do feel better, but you don't want to go to the Delta in the morning, that's fine. If you begin to feel worse, our driver can take you to the clinic, okay?" She looks at me skeptically. I know she despises the idea of going to the clinic more than the fact that she might have malaria.

"Okay." She acquiesces. She climbs down from the truck like an angry gymnast. She then climbs into her tent like one clearly without malaria. I'm really hoping she has ibuprofen in there.

After dinner I check on her as she has skipped it, which is nothing unusual for her. "How's it going in there?" I ask. She doesn't unzip the tent.

"I not going to the Derta," she says.

"How about the clinic?" I ask with a smile.

"No crinic," she says.

I do not want her to miss the Delta unless absolutely necessary. The idea of her not being there, however, is very attractive as she is one I would definitely need to keep an eye on in the wilds of the Okavango.

"I'll tell you what. If you aren't feeling better tonight, my tent is right over there. You come and get me and I'll take you to the clinic. If you sleep, we can wait till morning. I will come and check on you. If you are feeling better, then you will come, okay? You really shouldn't miss the Delta. Even if you're not 100 percent, you can rest there, which it exactly what you'd do here but without all of us." There is silence, and once again I fear she hasn't understood me. "Hae Soon?"

"I heal you, Mat. You arways think I don't heal you but I do!" she yells.

I shake my head. "Is that the plan then?" I ask cordially.

"Yes," she says quietly.

"Come get me if you need me," I say and walk away before I blow a gasket.

At 6:20 a.m. she has yet to emerge from the tent. She is usually late but this morning we are leaving at 6:45 a.m., and everything has to be packed and ready including our tents. I tap on her tent. "Hae Soon? Are you up?" I hear her moving around inside the tent. I'm picturing the raincoat covering her ears so she can't hear me. I shake the tent a little more.

"I'm okay. I'm hele," she says.

"How do you feel?" I ask. She moves some stuff around her tent. *Does exasperating mean anything to you?* "How are you feeling, Hae Soon. Do you feel better than last night?"

"Nope," she says. "I feel much wolse."

I feel for her. She is going to have to stay and go to the clinic with our driver, Cliff. She will not enjoy that experience. I open my mouth to tell her so but she interrupts me with, "I feer much wolse, but much bettel than yestelday." *Rrrrrr.* I keep myself together but am more than ready to leave her behind. "I'm glad to hear it, Hae Soon," I say with as much equanimity as possible. "Are you coming then to the Delta?" I ask.

"Yes," she says as if there was never a doubt.

"We're leaving in fifteen minutes so please have your stuff ready." She doesn't respond, and I walk away doing breathing exercises to keep from having a heart attack.

A day and a half later, I awaken from my nap at 3:00 in the afternoon before our afternoon hike or Delta boat cruise. I unzip the front of my tent and stand in the opening. I have put my tent completely on the other side of our encampment and separated from everyone else by a copse of trees. I always do this so that there is a greater chance of having animals come much closer to my tent during the night. I walk from my tent and follow the short path to the camp where everyone is relaxing.

Kyle, a funny, thirty-something from England walks by me on his way to the toilet. He stops me.

"Hey, mate. Did you see Hae Soon?" he asks.

TRIALS AND TRIBULATIONS

I immediately get a queasy feeling in my stomach. "Not since this morning, why?"

He shakes his head and frowns. "Mate, that girl just walked by me on my way from the toilet. She was headed out there." He points out toward my tent and the great beyond. My immediate anger turns to a bolt of fear.

No one is allowed to venture outside the campsite without the accompaniment of a Botswanan guide or myself. Staying in the camp is mandatory, without argument. I said it repeatedly to my clients including, Hae Soon, to whom I said it even more deliberately. This prohibition is quite obviously due to the fact that we are camping in the true wilds of Africa and surrounded by some of the world's deadliest animals. For Exhibit A, we had seen elephants browsing several hundred yards out from the camp in the exact direction in which Hae Soon has apparently ventured.

"Unbelievable," I say.

"What's unbelievable is that girl has made it to her twenties!" Kyle says.

I couldn't agree more. The problem is she may not make it to this evening. I race back through the trees to the clearing. I scan the distance for the characteristic green raincoat. I spot the elephants way off to my right, a thousand yards out. I continue scanning until I see her figure stand up from the ground in a small copse of mopane trees five hundred yards out from the camp. I take in a deep breath and exhale. "*Thank whatever powers there be...*" She is equally far from the elephants, a fact for which I am also grateful. It doesn't mean, however, there aren't a host of other animals stalking her at this very moment. I break into a fast jog beelining for her delicate figure in the distance. As I'm running, I'm thinking of killing her myself.

"Hi, Mat," she says nonchalantly as I reach her, my eyes scanning the trees, bushes, and grasses spreading out from us in every direction. She holds up a small bouquet of flowers to show me. "Pletty

65

frowels," she says and smiles. I'm too thankful for the fact that she isn't a carcass being chewed on by any number of predators to yell at her. It is at this point that I realize that she is someone who may need my compassion rather than my anger.

She is obviously one of those of people who has been raised in a closet and/or was born totally and completely without any common sense, or, I might add, an ability to understand English but speak it very well. Judging from her own self-description, I may even have to chalk her up to being an idiot-savant. "You can't be out here, Hae Soon. We have to go back to the campsite." She smiles at me as if she had no understanding of why we couldn't be out this far from the camp. It occurs to me that she is probably an amazing pianist.

We chat our way back to the campsite, my eyes darting here and there all the way to make sure nothing may be trailing us. The elephants are still busy, too far away for us to worry about them. She talks more than she ever has, telling about how she became a pianist. I am amazed she has so little cluelessness about her cluelessness. I realize in that moment she is like a twenty-six-year-old child and needs more compassion than judgment.

The trip has ended, and we are in Victoria Falls, five days after the Delta fiasco. Lisa, a twenty-two-year-old from Miami, runs up to me completely exasperated. "You're not going to believe what happened with Hae Soon at the Falls!"

Somehow, I think I'm going to believe it. "What happened? Is she all right?"

"Holy s—t! She's okay *now*! She almost went off the cliff!" I'm already thinking I wished I hadn't asked. "She was with us, and you know that part that says stay off the rocks, well, she didn't!" That sounds about right to me. Although she says she can read, it doesn't mean it was comprehended or processed.

"We kept telling her to stay away from the rocks and the edge but she wouldn't listen. We went a little farther down from her, and we heard her scream. We ran back to her, and she had slipped on the rocks and was right at the edge of the cliff! That girl is a maniac!" I couldn't agree with Lisa more.

"Is she hurt at all?" I ask. "Not at all."

Lisa says, "She was laughing. It's amazing that girl has made it to this age!"

Funny how there seems to be a consensus on this observation. "Glad she made it," I say. "Thanks for saving her."

Lisa shakes her head. "That girl is a maniac!" She adds one more time.

Later I find Hae Soon at her tent, rearranging her things for packing. She is leaving the next day, but it occurs to me I don't know what she is doing. "Are you all right?" I ask her. She doesn't know what I'm talking about. "Lisa says you fell at the Falls. Are you hurt?"

She laughs. "I fine, Mat. I farr down arr the time. It's nothing."

If it's nothing to her, it's nothing to me. I fight to keep myself from asking what she's doing now that the trip has ended. I have a feeling I'm not going to like what she has to say and when she says it, I'm going to feel compelled to help her.

"Are you flying out tomorrow?" I ask, dreading the answer.

"Oh, no," she says. I take tlain to Dal es Saraam tomollow and then to Zanzibal." I close my eyes and consider how much of my codependent self I want involved here. Hae Soon's senselessness seems to have a somewhat suicidal tinge to it. Traveling to Dar es Salaam by train, by herself, smacks of certain doom for her.

She would have to take a taxi from the border to Livingstone, Zambia. She would then have to take a bus to Lusaka, which is a city that isn't exactly known for its tourist-friendly logistical qualities. She then would have to find a place to stay as the train wouldn't leave until the next day. She would then have to take the train for a couple days if it doesn't break down all the way to Dar. There she would need to take another taxi to a place to stay and then find her way to Zanzibar by boat. She may as well be a blind mouse in a maze filled with hungry cats. I tell myself that her trip ended this morning and she is no longer my problem. She has made it twenty-six years without my help. She can make it another week by herself. Except, she's in Africa. I exhale a cloud of defeat and shake my head above her as she packs her bag.

"What time are you leaving tomorrow?" I ask.

"I think I take taxi at ereven with the Amelicans to the boldel," she says.

Just for giggles I ask her, "And after that?"

She doesn't flinch. "Oh, I get taxi on othel side to town," she says.

"Do you know where you're staying?" I ask her. "No. I find hoster ovel thele."

She is going to die is all I can think. I sigh. "Let me look into a few things for you, okay? I will come meet you at ten-thirty at the reception and have an itinerary for you. "Okay?"

She smiles at me. "Yes. Thank you, Mat. You vely good guide," she says. I walk away, shaking my head for the umpteenth time. I have a bit of work to do to make sure she has people meeting her at every stage of her journey.

I call Simba at Wild Horizons and he finds me taxis for her on this side of the Falls. I make her a reservation at a backpackers' in Livingstone and have them pick her up on the Livingstone side. The representative at the backpackers is extremely helpful. She can get Hae Soon on a bus and get her to Lusaka where a worker at a sister hostel will get her at the bus stop and take her to the train station. I call my contact, Bashir, in Dar es Salaam, Tanzania, who gets us our ferry tickets to Zanzibar. He has contacts everywhere and explains the situation. He assures me not to worry that he will handle everything only that she must call him when she gets on the train to Dar.

I thank him profusely and explain to him how he is saving a life. I feel much better now that Hae Soon will be met all along the way.

The next day, I check my watch at 10:25 a.m. and head toward the reception. I have all the information for her written down and ready to hand to her. I'm feeling pretty good about the whole thing as she will most likely survive this trip given what is planned for her. I am more than a little relieved that she hasn't died on this trip already and will most likely not die on the rest of her trip. When I reach the reception area, the Americans are standing there with their bags waiting for their taxi. I smile at them, and we chat.

After twenty minutes and no Hae Soon, I go into the reception area to check if maybe she is hiding in there. She isn't. I ask at the front desk if they have seen her. They have not. I walk back out to Lisa. "Heh, have you seen Hae Soon? She was supposed to meet me here before leaving."

"Yeah. She was here but she left just before you came here."

My jaw drops. "What?" I ask, stunned.

"Why? Did you have something for her?" Lisa asks.

I burst out laughing. What do they say about insanity? Doing something over and over that gets one result and expecting a different one. I shake my head. "No," I say. "I have nothing for her." I tear up her itinerary and list of numbers. "God, I hope she makes it."

POSTSCRIPT

Over the next few months, I wonder if Hae Soon actually made it to Dar. I never hear anything from anyone about her. I don't get any apocryphal tales or news bytes about a young South Korean jazz pianist missing from East or Southern Africa. What I do get, six months later, is a friend request on Facebook. Looking at Hae Soon's smiley profile picture I shake my head for the last time in this lifetime about her. This is a girl who has truly defied Darwin's most cherished principles.

HANZ

"I want you to know that this story was told to me by the driver I trained with, Alouise, with whom I worked during my first months in overlanding. He swore it's true, and it is *so* absurd that it can only *be* true. Even if it isn't true, it is still a wonderful, cautionary tale that I hope you will all take to heart and body before we go out into the wilds of Africa," I say as I begin my speech about being out in the wilds of Africa.

"Hanz is a thirty-something German guy, handsome, capable, successful, and, extremely arrogant. He touts himself as a soon-to-be professional photographer. He has defied everything the driver, the cook, and the guide have told him consistently throughout his forty-two-day adventure from Cape Town to Nairobi. His first real transgression occurred at the campsite, Rainbow Lodge on the Kavango River that separates Namibia from Angola. The campsite sits right on the river and sometimes at night, the hippos come out of the water to graze on the short grasses in the campsite. Hanz is told, like everyone present, *not* to try and take photos or bother the hippos if they enter the campsite during the night. Hippos are known to hold the reigning title of greatest killers of human beings of any of the large African animals.

"Hanz, however, had other ideas. In the middle of the night a hippo came into the campsite. Instead of staying in his tent and ignoring it, Hanz grabbed his camera and decided to follow it around in order to take photos of it. The hippo also had other ideas and decided to try and kill Hanz. They found Hanz in a tree the next morning where the hippo had kept him the whole night." People usually laugh at this, which is a good thing. It warms them up for the grand finale of Hanz's Darwinian misadventure.

"You would think Hanz would have learned his lesson, but, in fact, he did not. When they reached Arusha, Alouise sees Hanz buying meat from a street vendor. Alouise knows that Hanz knows not to buy meat from a street vendor so he finds it very strange. He finds it even stranger when he later sees Hanz give his package of meat to the cook, Edmund. At Hanz's request, Edmund places it in the cooler, on ice, with the meat for the truck."

"When it is time to leave for the Serengeti, Alouise sees Hanz packing his stuff into the Land Cruiser. Included with his paraphernalia is the aforementioned package of meat, his camera equipment with a tripod, and above all weirdness, a *fishing pole*. It is not Alouise's job to ask questions of the clients so he says nothing."

"When they set up camp, Hanz sets up his tent along the perimeter of the campsite. At night when everyone has gone to sleep, Hanz sets up his tripod at the screen of his tent. He takes his fishing pole out and his package of meat. He hooks a slab of meat to the fishing hook. He then casts the meat out into the open middle of the campsite to see what it might attract. He then climbs into the tent and leaves the screen partially open so he may take photos. He sets himself behind the camera, his feet hanging just outside the tent. After less than fifteen minutes, the bloody meat has a taker. It is a spotted hyena out on the prowl."

Most people at this point are staring at me with their mouths wide open or shaking their heads with the *tsk-tsk* expression on their incredulous faces and for good reason.

"Hanz settles himself behind his camera and focuses it for a close-up shot. As the hyena smells the meat and begins nibbling, Hanz reels it in. Closer and closer he reels the unsuspecting hyena, all the way to the front of the tent. When the hyena is two feet in front of the tent screen, Hanz lays the fishing pole down and moves to the camera to get his cherished photos. That is when the hyena decides that a slice of meat may not be as tasty as Hanz. The hyena jumps forward and bites Hanz's toes and most of the top of his left foot off."

At this point most people are staring at me in abject horror or laughing, which is a good thing. After all, this is a cautionary tale and meant to be very dissuasive and unquestionably memorable.

"Needless to say, Hanz's screaming woke the campsite. He also succeeded in scaring off the hyena that decided to abscond with Hanz's digits. The guides tended to Hanz as best they could. They then decided that Hanz probably needed a thirty-thousand-dollar helicopter ride to remove Hanz from the Serengeti, his trip, and Africa as well."

I give them a moment to digest the gist of what I'm saying to them. "Any questions?" There are rarely any questions. This is a story that needs no explanation. "No? Okay, then the lessons are quite simple: First, doing stupid things like Hanz in the African wilds gets you into trouble. Second, don't be a Hanz and this will be the best time, ever."

TOMORROW IS ANOTHER DAY

"Tomorrow is a new day." How many times have I heard this expression, perhaps even considered it and meant to convey it to heart and mind as a practice, yet did not practice this wisdom at all? Many wisdom gurus suggest to us that one of our greatest failures of living is our inability to see today and tomorrow as any different from yesterday. We live "today" as if it were "yesterday." In fact, it is this lack of perspective that solidifies our mistakes and concretizes our habits, often to our detriment and continued suffering.

I wake up at Ulovane ready for my rifle-handling test, yet again. The past three months at Leeuwenbosch Lodge, where I have been working off my required ninety days of guiding for my Level Two, I have been taking Uncle Bill's *Swift* rifle from the locker and making it an essential part of my everyday workout. Between my sets of sit-ups and push-ups, I would take up the heavy rifle and go through the four exercises necessary for the passing of the Trail's Guide shooting test, obviously without bullets. I would do each exercise anywhere from five to ten times in a row, aiming at a little dot on the wall, racking up hours of rifle-handling. I got it down to an absolute science. I shaved a quarter of the time off my exercises. I could do them smooth as silk, my aim impeccable on that dot on the wall. There was no way I was going to fail the shooting test again. I know no work is enough until I achieve what is necessary to fulfill the dream. In my case, of course, the dream is the right and license to do *walking safaris*.

I am feeling the pressure that time is waning here at Ulovane, as I really only have five weeks left of the program, four of which I have to work. That doesn't leave any time for another shot (pun intended) at my rifle handling. On top of the pressure to get the shooting done, I also have ten approaches on dangerous game, or walking safaris, to do after I conquer the rifle-handling. If I don't pass the test, I might get another chance to do rifle-handling my week off just before the December fifteenth graduation, but I definitely won't be able to do the approaches before I have to leave. A serious dilemma, only answerable by nothing short of unequivocal success.

After a very small breakfast suitable for one with a fluttering stomach, I and five of the eight, one-year students, pack up the Land Rover with Pieter, the head of our program. We then head off to the very familiar rifle range deep in the recesses of the cattle farm owned by Woodbury Lodge's owner across the N2 highway from Amakhala. On the way, I assure myself that I have done the proper work, put in the time, and *nothing* could possibly deter me from my goal, not even the massive kick of the .375 rifle, which deeply bruised my biceps tendon the first time I used it.

We arrive and set up the rifle range. As I set up the targets the specter of doubt visits me. *What if I fail? I won't have the time to do it again. If I do fail, I will have to come back here and do it again, which will cost me unknown thousands and precious time in my life. The truth is, the odds are against me as qualifying is a matter of not inches, but* millimeters. *Less than millimeters. Less than 30 percent of every class at Ulovane passed the rifle-handling.What if the weather is windy?What if the sun is in my eyes?What if the rifle malfunctions?What if?…What if…What if?…*I block it out as best as I can as I wait for the firing to begin. I shadow-box, do jumping jacks, and focus on that little dot on wall in my mind as the target. I picture the specter of doubt at the end of the rifle's barrel. That helps. The specter dissipates. I am *ready*. Three months of incessant practice, it will be *instinctive*.

We set up the range for the first two exercises. The first exercise is to load the rifle from a resting position and bring it to firing position in fifteen seconds. The second called the "leopard charge" starts with the rifle in the left hand. One must swing it up to firing position while cocking it, fire three rounds into three separate targets, the first at fifteen meters, the second at ten meters, and the third at five meters. This is due to the rather awkward reality that leopards charge at an angle. One must then load the rifle again and aim it at a fourth, phantom target. This must be done in twenty-four seconds with perfect "rifle-handling" techniques.

These techniques are such things as not dropping any bullets, cleaning them if you do before reloading them, being safe (i.e. not pointing the weapon at anyone), checking to see your firing pin is relaxed when one has loaded the rifle *without* a bullet in the chamber, and, what I learned far too late, *one must use an open palm when utilizing the bolt*!You need thirty points in all. If you pass the first two exercises, you achieve the level of "vehicle-bound license."You may carry a rifle in a vehicle, which is a requirement for most reserves, if not all of them. I have never failed the first two exercises. If you pass the others you achieve the right to do walking safaris as lead rifle.

"Who wants to go first?" Pieter asks from his table just behind the firing line. I have always gone first whenever we have done rifle-handling. This is simply because I hate waiting with all that fluttering going on inside and most others dread it. "I will, if no one else wants to go." The head shakes are like Weeble-Wobbles all around. It is quite evident *no one* wants to go first. I take the hint and walk straight up to the table. I pick up the rifle, surprisingly much lighter than the one I'd been practicing with, and grip it in my hands. I smile. It feels so familiar, like a tennis racquet. *Like an extension of my body.* The butterflies dissipate.

There is no way I am *not* going to pass. I begin the preparations by checking the rounds, the rifle, and placing the rounds where I normally would in the elastic holder on the rifle's butt. Pieter hands me the blindfold. I put it on like I would a badge of honor built just for my head. "The rifle must be in stage one," Pieter reminds me.

I nod and grasp the bolt with my fingers closed, fist-like. I close it with an expert snap. I then snap the bolt shut using only my right forefinger and thumb. This is a little trick movement that usually requires the left hand to hold the trigger down while the right hand closes the bolt. A voice calls out from behind Pieter. "*You have to use both hands to close the bolt, Mat. You also have to use an open palm or you are going to lose points!*"

Pieter and I turn to look at the source of the warning. Emma, stands back behind me a dozen yards and off to the side, a "rifle Gestapo." She means well, but I'm not terribly pleased with the interruption. I look at Pieter. "She's right, Mat. You will lose points if you don't do it properly."

I blink at him. The full impact of what he's saying isn't quite registering. The effect of the brain not *wanting* to accept the reality is in full effect. I put the rifle down and stare at Pieter. "You're telling me *now* that if I don't use an *open palm* to lock and unlock the bolt during shooting I am *going to lose points?*" He nods in the affirmative. The horror breaks on me like a hurricane on my morning sea. *I am going to fail.* I have been practicing *the wrong way*. I have made instinctive what should be an entirely different movement. I darken visibly.

"Why didn't you tell us this before?"

Pieter looks at me objectively. "FGASA requires an open palm, Mat."

"Pieter, I have been practicing my rifle-handling everyday for three months for hours. The same movements every time, over, and over, and over, and over again. There is *no way* I'm going to be able to use an open palm!" I say with barely contained rage.

"Try your best, Mat," Pieter says, sympathetic to my cause but unable to help. Suddenly, I have an understanding of what Hell must be:

You work impossibly hard to develop as close to absolute hope as possible. It is then stripped from you in an instant with a ridiculous rule that nullifies all you have striven for, thus annihilating your hope.

"How many points do I lose if I use my closed hand?" I ask stoically. Truthfully, I want to cry my heart out. "Minus five points," Pieter responds. I take a deep breath. All I need is the time (ten points), two bull's eyes, and a five for the second exercise. If I practiced aiming at the dot on the wall correctly, it will translate perfectly to the targets.

I pick up the rifle for the loading exercise. I take a deep breath. *You're going to be fine, Mat.* I think to myself. I check my rounds and prepare. I actually haven't loaded a rifle in three months. Fifteen seconds is a long time for this as I remember. "I'm ready," I say.

I launch into action. I take my time grabbing the bullets and loading them. It is when you rush that you lose time by fumbling. I am totally at peace when I load it. I load easily and then aim the rifle. *Smooth, smooth, smooth.*

"You may unload," Pieter says. I do so and lay the rifle down in front of Schalk. "Eleven seconds on the dot." Pieter looks at the watch.

Good, I think. One down, another to go for the first two exercises. I look at Pieter and he looks at me seriously. "Watch your hand, Mat.

You will lose five points for it if you close the hand." I know he says it to be helpful, but it instantly infuriates me. I never had to focus on that before. I will have to now *not focus* on it.

I put on the earmuffs for deafening the roar of the rifle. I then methodically pick up the rifle. I take a deep breath and face the targets. Instead of just relying on my well-practiced instinct I am thinking, *Open palm, open palm, open palm.*

"Are you ready?" I hear Pieter yell. I am not ready. I want to scream about the injustice of it, but I hold up my thumb anyway. "Go!" Pieter yells again.

I launch into the exercise concentrating on the open palm. The going is slow and awkward, yet I hit a ten on the fifteen meter. I open palm the bolt for the second shot. Not used to it, I do it too hard. My next bullet jumps from the magazine onto the ground. *F--k!* I scream inside. I crouch down and grab the bullet. I wipe it on my shirt. I jam it back into the magazine. With an open palm I cock it again. I fire at the ten-meter target. My heart sinks into my stomach. I barely hit inside the circle. I open palm the bolt and shove it closed. *Boom!* I shoot the five-meter through the ten. I open palm the bolt and then reload the rifle. I aim.

"You may unload the rifle!" Pieter bades me. I stand there a second longer. I know I didn't make it on this exercise, one I have never failed before. Maybe there is hope...

We walk out to the targets and check them. I have a ten at fifteen meters, a two at ten meters, and a ten at five meters. If I have it in time, I will have a thirty-two. I need a thirty-five. I start to boil inside. It's probably a good thing at that moment I have put the rifle down. Three months for nothing. The dream will remain beyond my wanton grasp. "*Pull it together, Dry.*" My will cautions. "*You can do this. Forget the open palm and get the bull's-eyes. With time you will have forty as you should be getting anyway. It should be a bull's-eye every time.*"

Pieter sits and looks at the watch. "Twelve point three seconds." It is impossible. "That's not possible, Schalk. It took me eleven seconds to load it in the last exercise." Pieter looks a little baffled as well. "That's what the watch says. It doesn't matter. You had the open palm but dropping the bullet takes five off the score. You had a thirty-two target score. That leaves twenty-seven. You ready to try again?"

I can barely keep myself from screaming. I turn away for a moment. I can't remember the last time I have been so enraged, disappointed, and hopeless. It feels *clinically* incapacitating. *Pull it together, Mat! Pull it together, Mat! Pull it together!* I say to myself. I take another deep breath. I wait three seconds and exhale. I turn back to Pieter but I know before I touch the rifle, I'm done. I'll be lucky to hit the hill behind the targets.

"Mat, do you want to take a moment?" Pieter asks.

I grit my teeth. All I want in the world at that moment is to pass this test. I shake my head. "I'm taking the hit on the next one, Pieter. I can't do this with an open palm," I say more as a plead than a statement of fact. He nods, understanding all to well.

He almost pleads back. "Just concentrate on the open palm, Mat."

The first shot at fifteen meters isn't even close. It looks like a five. I bite down hard and flip the bolt closed hand like I practiced. I'm too quick on the second shot. I look at the target and know immediately I am done. It's off the target. A zero. I have failed again. The dream is postponed. I can't hold it in. I shoot the five-meter target not even aiming. It's a ten. I almost don't bother reloading. *"You f--king failed!"* I scream from the very depths of a possibly broken dream.

When I put the rifle down I can't look at Pieter or anyone else. He looks at the stop watch. "Very good time," he says, offering me a silver lining. It doesn't matter. He goes out and collects the targets. I stand there fuming. He tabulates everything and tries not to frown. "Twenty," he says flatly.

"I'm done, Pieter. I'm going back to the camp."

"You can still practice the other exercises, Mat," he says.

"No," I respond. "I'm outta here." I start to walk around the table.

"Remember, Mat, you have tomorrow to try again."

I don't respond. Without looking at the others, I grab my backpack, sling it to my back, and slink away from the range like a fatally wounded animal.

The walk back is an exercise in self-flagellation. I recount the failures in my life from my unsuccessful tennis career to tests I've failed to relationships into which I didn't put the effort I should have. With every step I sink further and further into self-pity, condemnation, and misery. By the time I reach the camp, a good four miles later, I am "bubblegum stuck to the bottom of the shoe of existence."

I crawl into the bed in my tiny room and wish the world to go away. What is life if you can't fulfill your dream? What if my tomorrow is another exercise in failing this part of my dream? I have spent countless hours muscle-memorying myself into assured failure not success. How can I possibly do any differently tomorrow? I fall asleep, curled into a fetal ball of psychic agony.

I wake three hours later, more exhausted than I when I crawled into bed. I lay looking at the ceiling. *Where do I go from here?* Without my Trail's Guide I am severely limited in an already limited industry. This is due to the fact that Southern Africa wants its own citizens to get its jobs, which is more than fair considering its overwhelming poverty and unemployment. I will never be allowed on the ground to show people what is under the rocks as well as in the bushes, what I love most.

I read for two hours and venture out into the lodge. The three-month students are there and ask me how I did. I mumble something about failing yet again, and they can see it isn't a subject I want to discuss. Twenty minutes later, the one-years are back from the range. Four of the five are ecstatic and begin telling of their successes. Emma actually passed the whole thing on her first try. *Very impressive.* I guess she had an open palm. I am surprised by my happiness for her. I thought for sure I would hate anyone who passed without the same suffering.

Pieter walks over to me. "How are you doing, Mr. Mat?" he asks.

"Dandy" is my unenthusiastic reply.

He laughs. "I have to thank you," he says. I look at him perplexed. "You *reeeeally* set the fire under these guys butts when you stormed off!" He laughs. "When you left, these guys were staring with eyes wide open! When they got to the line to shoot, they were scared stiff and shot beautifully!" I don't know whether I should punch him in the head or laugh. Pieter leans into and says with dead seriousness, "Tomorrow is another day."

There it is, like an old friend. *Tomorrow is another day*. As soon as he says it, something stirs in me. Perhaps it is that old willpower that has kept me going to this day through all the hardships and failures. Maybe it is simply the truth inherent in the statement that stirs me. I can bury myself in my self-pitying BS or I can hold onto something pure like this truth. How will I see myself tomorrow at this time if I succeed where today I failed?

I awake at 5:00 a.m. and cannot wait to get to the rifle range. Today, only Pam and I will be shooting so it will be a little more relaxed with less distractions. I have spent the whole night figuring out my plan of attack and I go over it as we drive to the site. I have a plan. When I get to the site, I warm up yet again with my usual regimen. The fluttering is gone. My stomach is filled with a grim determination that will not allow butterflies to prosper.

Pieter asks us who wants to go first. I feel like I should try something different for once. I tell them "Ladies, first, unless you want me to go first." Pam is steely-eyed. "I'll go first." We set up the targets. Pieter repeats the exercises with us and lets us practice them without actual shooting.

"Ready?" Pieter asks. We are. I back up and Pam takes her position.

For her first time shooting, Pam does all right. She passes the first exercise with little trouble. She just misses her time by a second or two on the second. Her aim is very good, however. She will have to do rifle-handling again, but she is pleased with her general result. Like me, when I arrived, she has never shot a rifle. The rest of the exercises will be practice for her. Her retrial will be in another week's time. "Good luck," she says, knowing what it means to me.

"Are you ready to do it this time, Mr. Mat?" Pieter asks with a smile.

"Today is a new day," I say with a smile back. I am surprised by my equanimity. I don't want it less. I just know I have a plan: I will try the open palm and take my time. If I fail on my second attempt it will be the way I practiced with taking the extra time to aim perfectly to make up for the loss of the five points. Every shot will be the dot on the wall.

I pass the loading in a couple seconds less than yesterday. I then ready myself for the next exercise at fifteen meters, ten meters, and five meters. Again the rifle feels an extension of my body. I have complete confidence again. *Today is a new day*.

"Go!" Pieter yells.

BOOM! Open palm! BOOM! Open palm! BOOM! Open palm! Reload. Open palm! Aim. I smile at the targets over my sight. There are two bull's eyes and a seven. My timing is great, I can feel it. I put the rifle down and Schalk smiles at me. "That is *much* better!"

My turn at canting, the exercise I have failed every time. It is the one I have failed now over six times. One bullet of three in the chamber at ten meters is a hanging fire (a bullet that fails to fire). When the rifle clicks with the "dummy bullet" one must turn the rifle over and eject the bullet. One must then fire until the magazine is empty, reload, and fire the third shot. This must be done in twenty-four seconds to get Trail's Guide Lead Rifle. It is the one exercise that I have practiced more than any other.

"Go!" Pieter announces.

Open palmed, I go through the drill. When the smoke clears I see the targets. I smile. With an open palm I have hit my targets. It is two bull's-eyes and a five (oops). I smile as I know I have passed, finally. We come back to check the time. "Twenty-seven point three seconds," Pieter says. The pang of disappointment nearly kills me. Pieter looks at me to save me from that fate. "Good enough for intermediate. You passed, but you need to get better for Trail's Guide. Come on, Mat. Try again, and *do it* this time."

I nod at him. I look down at the rifle. I jump up and down. My plan is going into effect. I take the hit with the closed hand and concentrate on my bull's-eyes. If I get thirty-five I will pass. I need under twenty-three seconds, two bull's eyes, and a five. I can do this the way I trained myself to do it.

I stand ready. "This is it," I say to myself. "Just don't think about it. You're wired for this to go perfectly. No open palm bulls--t. Do what you know." I take a deep breath and give Pieter the thumbs up.

"Go!"

I swing the rifle up, cock it, and fire. *BOOM*! It is a bull's-eye. I cock it again. *Click!* Hanging Fire! I cant the rifle and eject the bullet. I aim. *BOOM*! Another bull's-eye. I bring the rifle down and reload. *One more, Mat! One more*! I scream inside my head. I aim. *BOOM*! It isn't the prettiest of shots, but it is enough. Best of all, I know it is fast. More than fast enough. A warmth spreads through me. *Elation*.

I take my time taking off my earmuffs and putting the rifle down. I don't even follow Pieter and Pam to the targets. They collect them and come back to me at the table. Pieter smiles at me, for me. "Twenty-two seconds." I shoot a thirty-seven. "Watch your hand, Mat," Pieter says, but I know he doesn't care too much. "Minus five, but that still leaves you with thirty-two. You got Trail's with that one. Only the buffalo and the lion left."

"I've never failed the buffalo and only once on the lion in six tries." Pieter and Pam, funny enough, both knock on the table. "Don't say that!" they shriek in unison. I knock on my head. "I'm *going* to do it."

Pam nails the buffaloes ruthlessly her first attempt. In eight seconds, at twelve and eight meters, she has two perfect bull's-eyes. It is a perfect showing. She tries again and misses her first shot. The second is just outside the bull's-eye and beyond the one centimeter needed for five of ten. I congratulate her on her first go and assure her of her passing it next time. "Your turn, now, Mat. Show us how it's done," he says with a grin.

Once again, I nail the buffalo exercise. Two shots in 7.3 seconds. I smile at them and them at me. We have become a team, and it feels good to have them in my corner. *One more to go.* I believe it is the easiest one of all despite its odd set up and adrenaline pumping effect.

We set up the lion. It is a sled with a thirty-meter rope. One person holds onto the rope as the person with the rifle approaches with guests. As soon as the rifle-bearer hits the designated line, the rope tower takes off in the opposite direction behind the rifle bearer, dragging the sled. The lion sled thus approaches at the rate of the runner. The shooter must yell, "Stand still, don't run, stay behind me!" The shooter must then cock the rifle and yell at the approaching lion to scare it off. This will actually work far more often than not in the wild as most animals will mock charge rather than actually attack. One can only shoot when the lion is within ten meters. One must then go through a couple more actions to make sure the "guests" are okay, ensure the lion is dead, and the rifle is ready and safe.

I ask Pam if I can go first on this exercise. She graciously says yes. She smiles at me as she takes up the rope on the lion. "Good luck. This is it. Just one more shot."

"Thank you. Run very slow."

She laughs and readies herself.

I load the rifle and stand with Pieter. He is more ready for me to do this than I am I think. I go through the necessary directions for encountering anything in a dangerous situation. "Ready, Pieter?" He nods with a smile. He's done this seven times with me and who knows how many times with others. We walk...

I hit the line and Pam bolts. The sled shoots toward me. Although I know a lion would be charging at four times the rate of Pam, it is still impressive to see an angry lion face racing toward you. I hold my right hand back behind me to Pieter. "Stand still, don't run, stand behind me!" I yell. I raise the rifle as the adrenaline, as always, leaps into my veins. Thirty yards, twenty-five yards, twenty yards, the lion face races toward me. "*HEEEYAAAHHHH*!" I roar at the lion and take another step toward it. As it hits fifteen yards, I squat and take aim. I let the slavering face come closer, closer, closer and *BOOM*! I pull the trigger.

I immediately reload another bullet and cock it. I check the lion's pupil with the tip of the rifle to see that it is deceased. Once I've established the paper lion is indeed "dead", I unchamber the bullet. I check with Pieter, my client, to see that he is okay. He is smiling broadly at me.

I look down at the lion head between the eyes where the bull's-eye sits. There are a few other holes there from yesterday's shooting, but I know my shot is true. I also know my trials and tribulations are *done*. I almost burst into tears but smile hugely instead.

Pieter bends down to the sled and looks at the back of the lion picture. He pokes his finger in a hole. I look at it and smile. He looks at me very seriously. "That isn't your hole." The fear jumps up into my throat, and my face registers the shock.

"That *is* my hole," I insist, like he just told me the sky isn't blue.

He points to another hole, *far* above the lion's head, barely on the poster. He looks at me and I at him for a full three seconds. A grin crawls across his face. "I'm just kidding, Mat. That was from yesterday. Well done."

I laugh and almost burst into tears. I push him over. *Doesn't he realize I'm holding an elephant gun?*

It is *done. I am a Trails' Guide qualified Lead Rifle.* My today has nothing to do with all my yesterdays. That simple bit of wisdom has given me whole new tomorrows, all of them filled with my new dreams. I realize I just had to be willing to accept that I am not my yesterdays and my tomorrows will be other todays. *New todays, everyday...*

THE LION, THE DITCH, AND THE BONEHEAD

Not the lion area, I think grumpily to myself as I watch the wedding guests pile into the Land Rovers. As it is their last chance to game drive, they have insisted on seeing Amakhala's lions this afternoon. The horizon to the northwest beyond the lion area, however, looks like an ominous cataclysm of some sort is brewing. Judging by the massive cumulonimbus clouds present, we either are going to get a monster deluge, an alien invasion, or both within the next hour. In that, we are going to have to find our pride of five lions. *Five lions in eight-hundred hectares, parts of which have the densest pockets of woody-stemmed plants in the world.*

I'm grumpy not because of the terrible weather. I have happily been out game driving in weather they wouldn't allow on the lowest levels of Hell. But rather, I am clueless when it comes to the lion area. I always felt I would have plenty of time to learn the lion area in my first six months on the reserve before I started my next six months as a guide at Leeuwenbosch Lodge. The map of the lion area, one piece of paper stuck within a thousand other pieces of paper to learn while at Ulovane (my safari guiding school), kept getting pushed farther down the pile. Now, as I look from the guests excitedly piling themselves into the vehicle back to the doomsday sky, I'm wishing that paper had been on top until I'd learned it.

The map portrays the separate part of Amakhala Game Reserve where the lions are kept. The lions have to be there, for now, as the reserve is only ten years old. It isn't ready to have the apex predators mixed in with all the other animals. On any reserve, prey-species numbers must hit a certain self-sustaining population to survive predation. As Amakhala's five lions could easily eat over two-hundred animals a year, or one-sixth of Amakhala's total prey-species, the lions had to have their own area within which to hunt and live their lion lives before being introduced onto the main reserve. Thus, to keep them happy and hunting, Amakhala must continuously reintroduce animals into the lion area.

I am also grumpy because I have to lead my vehicle packed with ten guests *and* the vehicle behind me packed with another ten guests. This is due to the fact our new recruit, Donny, twenty-one, although a great kid and a fairly well-versed, Level One FGASA (Field Guide Association of Southern Africa) Safari Guide, is living his *second day* at Amakhala and knows absolute zero about the lion area. In other words, I am leading twenty-one people into an area I am about as familiar with as they are, but I have to make it look like I know *exactly* where I'm going.

The two things I have going for me is that thus far the clients have been thrilled about having their previous game drives with me, and they have no idea that I have no idea. I look over Donny already beginning his spiel about traveling in an open vehicle. He trusts me as he has been with me on a couple of drives over the past few days and seems to admire my knowledge and ability to connect with the guests. I'm incredibly glad he doesn't know the million ways I am trying to figure out how *not* to go into the lion area or make it look like we looked for them but didn't see them. Of course, on a Big Five reserve like Amakhala, there is huge pressure on the guides to make sure the clients get to see elephants, rhino, Cape buffalo, leopard, and especially the lions.

I look at the ominous thunderclouds moving toward us on the horizon one last time. "If you all look under your seats, you will find a blanket and a rain poncho there for you. It looks like we are going to get dumped on big time so feel free to use them accordingly." I'm hoping they will look at the sky and decide for hot chocolate by the lodge's fireplace. Some of the clients move to put the ponchos on already and I let them settle down before I begin my own spiel. They are *dedicated*. No one, to my chagrin, opts for hot chocolate and fireplace. *Ah, the love of lions.*

"Please make sure to keep your limbs inside the vehicle at all times. There is lots of vegetation here that can cut you up if any part of you is outside the vehicle. Please don't get off the vehicle unless instructed to do so by me. Also, please, keep your voices down as the animals can be annoyed by the sound of voices. In a sighting, please do not lean outside the vehicle to try and take a picture. The animals see the vehicles as a whole with interior moving parts. If you put anything outside the vehicle it will change the shape of the vehicle and they will be able to pinpoint you."

They are listening politely but I can see on their excited faces that they want to get this show on the road before we need to start building an ark. "Any questions?" I ask, looking at their eager faces.

"Let's go see some lions!" Jackie, a thirty-something guest from England squeals. I smile as genuinely as possible and slide into my seat. "Sh-t," I mutter under my breath.

As we head onto the reserve from the back gate of Leeuwenbosch, I get a brilliant idea. Janet, my fellow student and our eventual valedictorian in our one-year program, knows everything about everything. She had been assigned to Reed Valley, the lodge just down the road from Leeuwenbosch, which does day trips onto the reserve. As there is a great deal of pressure on the guides for day-trippers to see the lions, they almost always know where the lions are. I am praying that she will be on the radio. I pick up the radio and call in, "Mat for Janet, come in, Janet."

I know asking where the lions are is a little like cheating. Most clients want to try and find them or at least have a guide track them down by sniffing dandelions or tasting pebbles they believe were disturbed by the animals on their way to killing something huge. All I can think is *Desperate times require desperate measures.* "Janet here," comes over the radio. I clench a fist and my teeth. *Yes! We might actually see some lions today.* "Janet, I'm wondering if the lions have been located today at all," I query, trying my damn best to keep the relief I feel out of my voice.

"I'm just coming from them actually, Mat," she answers. I smile back at the people as a small cheer goes up from them.

The next thing she says fills me with the kind of horror one feels when goes from believing one is saved to utter damnation. "You know where the top of ----- is?" I know I have to answer her as everyone else behind me is listening to this conversation. "Uh, yeah, yeah." I respond hoping to convey to her telepathically that I have absolutely no idea where that is and if she would be so kind as to send me that exact location via the telepathic hotline that would be great. "Okay. Just go up there and pass the cisterns. Go down into ----- Valley and up the other side where ----- is, okay?" *No. It is categorically not okay, Janet, because I know I'm supposed to have learned all this during the first seven months of my being on the reserve, but everywhere you are describing may as well be in Foo-king, China!* "Go left up the hill there and follow the fence line. They are right there out in the open, all five of them. It is a perfect shot for the guests," she chirrups happily.

Small cheers break out behind me. Everyone in our truck and Donny's truck are stoked their guide now knows exactly where the lions are. All of a sudden I want to throw up. "Hey, thanks, Janet. That's great. Thanks so much," I manage to choke out. I think she gets that I may not be 100 percent certain, and she adds, "If you can't find them, I'll be on the radio, Mat." I hang up the radio with a flourish and look back at the guests with a huge grin, "Everybody ready for some *lions?*" A huge cheer goes up, and we head down the road to the lion area.

We stop at the top of the small hill that leads down to the tunnel. The tunnel runs one hundred yards beneath the N2, South Africa's largest southern highway, from Amakhala's safe-area (an area that is itself fenced in but not fenced from being in the reserve proper). This is to keep the lions, if they somehow found their way through the tunnel, from entering into the reserve and to contain them. The tunnel itself has a netting of electrified wire along the bottom of it to prevent anything from leaving the lion area. Nine thousand volts travel at intervals of three seconds through the wires, so anything that touches them will certainly think twice about trying to enter the tunnel again.

"Now remember, folks. In the lion area, the lions see you as part of the vehicle. Please no arms outside the vehicle and when we are near them, please keep your voices down." *It's not going to matter because we aren't going to see lions, but I'm telling you just in case some miracle happens and they fall out of the sky and land on the bonnet.* "There is no need to worry about the lions coming into the vehicle, but if one does come near, just stay very still and make no noise." Several of the faces are very grave. An open vehicle can indeed be a scary prospect when lions are concerned.

"Everyone ready?" I ask. Several excited nods indicate yes. I get a pang of guilt as I gun the engine in neutral for effect. I may have some disappointed guests because of my procrastination and that is unacceptable. I don't have time, however, to wallow in self-deprecation as Donny claps his hands and launches himself down into his seat. He's raring to see the lions for the first time, too.

I go to switch the vehicle into diff-lock but it won't go. I try it again but it won't take. *Sh-t. If this wasn't bad enough.* Diff-lock makes sure that all tires are working simultaneously so that if the vehicle gets stuck, they will all work to pull the vehicle out. The lion area is a morass of muddy valleys, streams, and rocky, steeply inclined roads. I'm definitely going to need it, if not only to get down the hill to the tunnel. I try it again, and it makes a horrible grinding noise. Some people clench their teeth and grip the bars in front of them. Forget it, I think. I'll get it later when the rains come. As we enter the tunnel, the drizzle starts.

As we exit the other side it is already raining. The cumulonimbus clouds are just off to our left looking like the harbingers of the End of Days. We drive up the long hill to get up to where the cisterns are located. The clients are completely covered and huddling against the pelting wind that has already begun to hit above twenty-five miles an hour. Not a religious person, I nonetheless find myself praying, *Please let me find these poor people some lions.*

At the cisterns, concrete water containers for the cows which used to inhabit the lion area, we stop for a decent view of the southeastern part of the lion area. I obfuscate the fact that from this point on we will be mostly lost by explaining the history of Amakhala and how Uncle Bill, the architect and visionary of Amakhala, went where no farmer was willing to go in building a game reserve from the farm that had kept his family fed and clothed their whole lives.

I scan the lion area with my binoculars through the huge raindrops as I *blah-blah*. On the inside I am still praying the felines will miraculously appear from the Shangri-la that Janet was previously describing. Donny, to his credit, also scans with his binos. We don't see any lions as I expected. Definitely worth the effort I deem as I put the binos away and clamber back behind the wheel. It at least has to look like I am trying.

I head northwest toward the corner of the fence where there is another great vantage point over the middle valleys of the lion area. My toes are crossed in my shoes as I scan the valleys. I can feel the clients thinking, *Didn't that other guide tell you exactly where they are?* I still want to make as good a show as possible and preempt this possible question. "I'm just checking around in case the lions have moved," I offer to the clients. They are looking more skeptical about our adventure then ever. I don't blame them. Lightning flashes across the vast expanse of the thunderclouds. Huge claps of thunder boom above us. I'm half-expecting an *Independence Day* spaceship to peek out from behind the clouds and begin laser beaming us.

When I see that the lions aren't going to help me out on this misadventure, I take a deep breath and sit back at the wheel. "Good! It looks like they haven't moved down into the valleys and the cover of the bushes here at least," I say as cheerfully as possible. Twenty eyes blink at me with a barely sustainable patience. I look over at Donny. He smiles broadly with his best teenage optimism and gives me the thumbs up. "Heh heh." I give him thumbs up back. *We're screwed.* I drop the Land Rover into gear and head down the road. I decide I will follow it to where I think Janet might be referring.

As our duo of vehicles rumble along, the rain begins to chuck down. Little rivulets begin to form on the hillside to our left, run onto the road, and continue down the hill to our right. If it becomes a deluge, this road is going to become a river. I put it out of my mind and focus on the road in front. I know there is a main road and a couple of short cuts to where I think Janet has told us the lions are, but the main road is farther down from the point where we are at present. I try entertaining the guests with the info I usually give when we are perusing the lions:

"A lot of people think male lions are lazy and females do all the hunting. The reality is a little different. Their relationship in a pride is a like a division of labor for which the male lion is ultimately rewarded by feeding first. He guards and marks the territory within which the pride lives. He fights off other lions and other predators from the territory. The females' job is to do the hunting. The truth of the matter is, the females don't really want a male hunting with them as he has a huge furry mane that is easily seen, and he is usually a third bigger than they are."

I'm pretty sure the people are humoring me as I can barely hear myself talking over the pounding of the rain on the roof and the hood of the Land Rover. I come to a point in the road where it curves to the right and I'm quite certain the place we want to be is to the left and behind us as the northern fence is no more than one hundred yards in front of me. I've definitely missed the shortcut. I almost burst into tears. I need to turn around, but Donny is behind me and in front of me is undrivable terrain becoming less drivable every minute as the water pours down the cracks and crevices in the road. I stop the vehicle. Donny follows suit behind me. "Excuse me a moment." I pick up the radio.

"Donny for Mat." I press into the radio. A bunch of incomprehensible static and garbled nonsense comes through. I wait for more but none comes. I try again. "Mat for Donny, come in," I say. Even less static comes in this time with even less nonsense. The static persists for four seconds and then silence. One of our radios is malfunctioning. *What else?* I think to myself. I lean out my door into the pouring rain and wave for him. Donny leans out, points at his radio and shrugs. I can barely hear him over the rain as he yells. "My radio's dead!" *Purrrrfect.*

"We need to turn around!" I yell to him. "We're going to follow the fence line and curve back to the left. That's where they are!" I yell over the rain. He waves and clambers back into the Land Rover. *Right, that's where they are.* It's going to take an absolute miracle to find them, and it is more than obvious now that I have no idea where I'm going or where the lions are.

Donny revs his engine behind us. He backs up and then cuts back left up the hill with a bump and a grind. He then sits there waiting for me. Unfortunately, he is exactly where I need to go but now I can't call him or gesture to him. I decide to brave the road in front of me for a few yards until there is a place I can turn around. I am definitely going to need all four wheels for this trick.

I look down at the diff lock and grit my teeth. *Please work*, I silently beg the handle as I grasp it. One, two, three, I jam into place and...*ker chunk*! I can feel my clients behind me jump. I try the clutch to see if we're ready to rock and roll. *Vrrrummm*! We categorically are not. *Rrrrrrr*. I smile back at them. "No problem!" I announce to them. The front row is frowning at me with clear disbelief. *I* don't believe me so why should they? I inch slowly forward to the cracks in the road trying to keep the tires aligned with the tops of the cracks. I try again. One, two, three, *ker chunk*! I put it into gear. *Vrrrummm*! *Forget it. I'm doing this with front-wheel drive from here on out!* I think to myself.

We bounce and slide and slide and bounce down the limestone-encrusted road. The tires make loud splashes as they fall into the small rivers running down through the crevices in the road. Everybody behind me is holding onto the bars and each other for dear life. We go like this for about twenty yards, me cursing vehemently on the inside. I reach a large guarrie tree, which blessedly has a small area next to it that will allow me to turn around. This much I do smoothly and easily. Now, I just have to go back up the cracks and crevices and rivulets to where Donny sits waiting in the rain.

When I reach Donny, I can see his people wear the same unhappy masks on their faces that my people are most assuredly wearing behind me. If I don't find lions in the next fifteen minutes, there might be a lynching before the wedding. I pass Donnie with an index finger pointing upward. I'm just happy he and his people don't respond with their middle fingers. As we ascend, I am not following a road to speak of, but I know regardless of the lions that we need to stay on high ground to avoid any flash floods on the roads.

We bounce and grind through bushes and rocks as I scan in every direction for lions. At this point everybody couldn't be much more miserable and neither could I. We reach the top of the hill and look out over the expanse of the farmland all around us with the "End of the World" sky above us. Lightning crackles across the sky and an "*Ohhhh!*" escapes someone's lips behind me. It is beautiful but not as beautiful as lions. I shake my head slightly. It is time to go back, lions or no. No sense in getting hit by lightning. As I turn to tell everyone behind me that we were going to give up and return home, as it is just too dangerous to be out here, Donny pulls up alongside of me.

"Heh, Mat. My client thinks she dropped her purse that has her business phone in it back down there on the road when we turned around. I'm going to go back down there and look for it." I shake my head at him. "No. Just follow me back. Maybe we can look for it later," I say to him. He shrugs and backs his Rover up to get back behind me. I look down and grab the radio.

"Leeuwenbosch for Mat, come in."

"Will here, Mat."

"Will, one of the clients in Donny's vehicle dropped her purse and phone somewhere on the road by the northern fence. We may need to come back and get it at some point. Can you pick the clients up on the Paterson Road entrance? I don't think the tunnel is a great idea as it must be flooded by now, no?" I ask calmly, trying to keep just how pear-shaped this has become from being apparent.

"I'll meet you there in twenty minutes with the van," Will responds and crackles off.

Twenty minutes? It's going to take me twenty minutes to find the road out of here. I replace the receiver and look at the pool of water growing in my crotch where the raincoat is no longer protecting me. *How the hell am I…?* "Lion!" Jim yells, just behind me. I look up from my reverie to where he's pointing.

Sure enough, not fifty yards from us is our male lion, Mufasa, looking wet and miserable. He walks from behind a bush and slouches over to Scar, our female, who just happens to be out in the open next to another bush fifty yards to our left. A huge cheer goes up. "You found them, Mat! Way to go, Mat! Great job!" It takes every ounce of willpower of mine not to burst out either laughing or crying. *Miracles do happen.* I have never been so happy to see an animal in my life. I drop the Land Rover into gear and chug forward to the cats.

Even as the thunder roars above us, the wind whips rainjackets around in the truck, and lightning lights up the ever-darkening sky, we take a few moments to admire Amakhala's lions. I look back at the faces behind me and everybody is riveted by these magnificent creatures as they should be. Mufasa is a perfect specimen of *Panthera leo*, Africa's most iconic big cat. Everybody is thrilled with our finding them. So am I. Apparently, all that time I spent moving the map farther down the paper pile, at least the general idea of the lion area stuck subconsciously.

After ten minutes and a hundred photos with rain-splashed cameras, most settle back in their seats. We need to go. It is turning into a hurricane out here. "Everyone happy with lions?" I ask. "Oh, yeah! Great! Amazing!" rings out over the roaring wind. "Let's get out of here," I say to them and start the engine. Mufasa gets up as if our engine were an invitation and walks stage right. I think he's probably going to find shelter after an hour of being pelted by icy raindrops. As I turn to head down the hill to the road I know is somewhere below us, I realize Donny is not with us.

I stop the vehicle and look behind us. I peer in every direction as far as I can see, but he is gone. The rookie has gone to get the purse after I told him not to and I can't call him to tell him not to go through the tunnel. *Sh----------------t!* He also doesn't know that we are supposed to meet Will at the side gate of the lion area. My only chance, I reason, is to head him off near the cistern on the way to the tunnel. That is, of course, if he remembers the way back. Just when I thought things were looking up…

We bounce down the hill for about a hundred yards and finally hit the road. I delicately maneuver the Land Rover onto the limestone and muddy water. I decide we'll need to put a little pedal to the metal to catch up to the kid if indeed he was on his way back toward the tunnel. I drop the stick into gear and rev the engine. I'm about to jet forward when Mufasa materializes from behind a tree just to the right of the road in front of us. The lion doesn't even deign to look back at us as he slinks his way onto the flooding road. Completely involuntarily, I burst out laughing. *You gotta be kidding me! Murphy wants to chuck me a lion now!*

Despite the fact that the wind is howling at thirty miles an hour, the rain is falling like the sky is falling, thunder is crashing like it wants to spilt the planet in half, and lightning is threatening all creatures out in the open with total electrical annihilation, Mufasa walks down the road with the nonchalance of a housecat after his evening meal. All I can think about is the truckful of people that are going to be trapped in the flooded tunnel with my young coworker on an electrical grid.

The cameras click over my shoulder as we follow Mufasa down the road at two miles an hour. I can't stop shaking my head. *I wonder what he'll do if I just bump him the slightest bit…*I don't want to honk at him as that might spook him. I can't go around him as there is the 45-degree hill on my right. On my left the land plummets to the valleys below. As long as this lion is in the road, we are staying right here.

One minute goes by. Two minutes go by. It is a full seven minutes of us following the swaying butt and testicles of the biggest male lion I have ever seen when Mufasa decides that he has had enough of the road and cuts left to go down into the valleys. It is the happiest I've ever been to see an animal disappear from sight. I step on it past him and gun it up the road.

When I reach the cisterns, Donny is nowhere to be seen, and I know he couldn't be back behind us unless he is completely lost in the lion area. I call Will on the radio.

"Will here."

I realize I don't quite know what to say. "Um, just out of curiosity, Will, could we use the tunnel to get back? I think Donny wants to use it."

"He's back at the lodge" is Will's flabbergasting statement.

"What?" is all I can say.

"Yeah. Donny took the tunnel back to the lodge. Just come meet me at the side gate like we decided. Will out."

That little rascal! I think. *Ha ha!* He found his way back by himself. *Good on you, Donny boy!*

When I reach the Paterson gate, the rain is an onslaught. I have never seen clients more happy to be saved from game-driving, including those who had been threatened by wild animals. Will, under the safety of an enormous umbrella, files everyone into the van. He shuts them in and comes over to me where I shiver in the icy puddle my seat has become.

"He didn't find the woman's phone, Mat," Will says with perfect equanimity.

"Shame," I respond as if this news flash has nothing to do with me.

"You have to go look for it," Will says. I look at him as if just told I'd be rocketing a spaceship to Mars.

"I'm sorry?" I say. *According to the sky, the End of Days is about to happen. I am driving around in a big metal box with wheels with lightning everywhere. I have absolutely no idea where this woman dropped her phone and I have to go back and find it?*

"Apparently her phone is quite important as she has a business call she needs to take," he says. "Donny said she dropped it back by the road where you turned around. Good luck."

Will strides back to the van, closes his monster umbrella, and climbs in. I think a whimper escapes me, but I can't be sure. The clients wave cheerfully at me from the van's windows. Will gives me a small salute and peels away back for the warm comfort of hot chocolate and the fireplace.

A huge crash of thunder shakes the earth and lightning crackles across the sky. I burst into laughter. This is nothing more than I deserve. If I had done my homework and known the lion area, Donny would have never had to make the turn that lost our client her phone. With perfect humility, I close the gates to the lion area behind me. I clamber into the rain-soaked vehicle and head back toward the area I think she has lost her pink purse. I am freezing and miserable but at peace after owning up to being a bonehead.

POSTSCRIPT

After two hours of braving Armageddon's weather, I don't find her pink purse or phone. I do, however, get some quality time to learn the lion area all by myself. I know I will never be lost in the lion area ever again, *ever*.

It is actually not until late morning the next day that the purse is found. Apparently, Scar likes pink purses as well. The guides find her purse in the lioness's clutches being chewed into a million pieces. Fortunately, the phone is unharmed, perhaps being saved for later chewing. They collect the purse and phone from the newly washed lioness. Our client makes her phone call. Apparently she gets a lot of extra credit for using a phone that an hour before was in the paws and jaws of an African lion.

Chapter One: Elephant Connections

Chasing Elephants at Midnight

Anz, Nora, and Phillip

<u>Twyfelfontein where we have spent the day is renowned for two
things, its cave paintings…and the desert elephants that live in the
stark dryness of Namibia's northwest…</u>

(photo by Anna Martin)

Chapter Two: Trials and Tribulations

<u>The Lion, the Ditch, and the Bonehead</u>

<u>Mufasa, different day</u>

(Photo by Schalk Pretorius)

<u>Mufasa, Scar, and the Cubs, different day</u>

(Photo by Schalk Pretorius)

Chapter Three: Dances with Whatevers

<u>Dances with Monitors</u>

<u>My back window faces the vast blue expanse of Lake Malawi</u>

Mat! There it is! There's that thing I saw this morning!

Heebie-Jeebies with Rain Spiders

I frown at her precarious position above the door…

Chapter Four: The Gift of Sharing Africa

Toilet Monitor

Playing dead has seemed to have worked thus far...

Muzungu in the Mist

Sitting in a dense pocket of thistle is a huge silverback...

(photo by Les Ash)

He slides momentarily until he halts his descent by grabbing onto some branches…

His huge domed head, massive shoulders, thick fur…pass by with only a side-long glance…

(photo by Brian Sinuk)

If Brian has made it here, ANYONE can…

<u>Not Your Average Cat</u>

<u>The lioness reaches the side of our car...</u>

(photo by Meredith Simcock)

Her ears are laid back as she peers around the back of a vehicle at her prey…

(photo by Meredith Simcock)

<u>She stands in the cloud of dust…waiting for the death twitching of the gazelle to subside…</u>

(photo by Meredith Simcock)

A Plea for Rhinos: Why We Need Them

These animals reach into the deepest parts of our hearts…
to remind us of something sacred…

(photo by Schalk Pretorius)

THE VANISHING

I sit on a stool watching the firelight dance on the 700-million-year-old reddish granite and gneiss of the kopje. Kopje literally means "little head" from the Dutch, and refers to the 600- to 1,000-foot-plus outcroppings that rise up from the Namibian desert floor at Spitzkoppe. We have come here not only for the splendor of Spitzkoppe itself, the several-thousand-year-old San paintings that are found here designating it as a place considered sacred by the Bushmen, and the extraordinary hiking and climbing the kopjes have to offer, but also for our talent show I host on every three-week trip's halfway point.

We wait for thirty-two-year-old Connor to come out for his turn in our show. This would be the second talent show for him, much to his chagrin. He is on the forty-two-day trip down from Nairobi to Cape Town and thus experiencing his second three weeks. I can't help but think back to his previous showing at the first three-week's talent show and what he claimed was his only talent.

Connor appeared on the "stage," which was the area around the campfire in the middle of our campsite on Lake Malawi, with three, twelve-ounce beer cans. He told us quite simply and dubiously. "Tis is moi only tahlent. It's cuz Oim Oirish." Connor emptied the contents of the beers into his face one immediately after the other. I thought it was an outstanding display of a particular talent, not one I would recommend for young people and/or people with cirrhosis of the liver to aspire to, but impressive still. I know if I attempted the same, I would most certainly either projectile vomit for an hour or die. After his beer-guzzling performance he disappeared behind the truck. We thought for certain he was going to throw up for an hour or die. We were astounded when he returned immediately clutching three more beers to carry him over for the rest of the show.

Here at Spitzkoppe, I'm thinking it is going to be a repeat performance or something similar. This is due to the fact that we did have quite a few new faces join us at Vic Falls on our way down and haven't yet seen his "only" talent. He already got kudos from the group who had witnessed his anomalous liver-defying presentation, thus it would make sense for him to attempt a repeat performance. A few snickers ring out from our crowd. They know he had already been quaffing a few before the show in order to gain some "liquid courage" as had a few others.

Everyone quiets down when Connor's voice rings out from behind the truck: "Hit it!" *Riverdance* music comes ringing out from the truck. Everyone instantly starts clapping as they recognize that Connor is going to pull out another "Oirish talent." This show, however, instantly promises something much more hilarious. We don't have to wait for the comedy of it.

Connor, shirtless, flings himself around the front of the truck and races to the stage. As he attempts to stop, his feet hit the slippery, graveled floor of our campsite between the kopjes. Connor overshoots the stage. He trips and hurtles headlong into a small acacia bush covered in thorns stage right. A loud "Oooooooo!" erupts from us knowing that had to hurt.

No one knows quite what to do as no one is certain if this was intentional or not, a sort of Irish, Charlie Chaplan effect. I, however, know all too well the degree of pain associated with falling face-first into an acacia bush. I half get up to extricate him if necessary. As if not wanting to be late for the rest of his performance, however, he flails himself wildly to extricate himself from the prickly embrace of the acacia. It looks painful, but everyone is too amused to worry. With blood streaming down a dozen scratches all over his torso, arms, face, and ear, Connor launches himself with wild abandon into his best version of Irish dancing à la Michael Flatley. I clap along with everyone despite the fact he looks like someone out of a battlefield scene in *Braveheart*. I'm hoping he is as drunk as I think he is.

The group is loving him. He is by no means a talented Irish dancer, but his genuine effort and enthusiasm is enough to charm everyone. If he had done a comedy routine, it wouldn't have been more amusing. When the music stops, we erupt in clapping and cheering and when the counting is done, it is already evident that Connor is in the final three. He sits down for the rest of the performances, beer in hand. People around him tend to his cuts and scratches with tissue and alcohol from the medical kit. I don't know if they need the alcohol as it might actually be running *from* his cuts. I'm a little worried about his right ear, which looks like he left a bit of it in the bush. I advise a little extra cleaning there.

Forty-five minutes and several talentless acts later, he clinches the win with a long Irish bar song. Although he doesn't have the best voice, he definitely has won the hearts of the group. Most people thought that drinking was his only talent, but he had been holding out on us along the way. As we crown him winner of the talent show, Vic and his trip girlfriend, Gina, come up to him and wrap their arms around him. "You're coming up there with us, right!"

"Of course!" is his bleary-eyed response.

"Up there" as Vic calls it, is the top of the kopje. It is the one place along this trip where it is safe for the clients to sleep outside without their tents. As everyone gathers his/her stuff to make the twenty-minute climb to the top of the two-hundred-fifty-yard tall kopje, the wind begins to pick up. I've already experienced some howling winds in this particular campsite in the past. It is strategically sandwiched between two of the larger kopjes at this point of the park. It forms a perfect wind canyon running north-south. If one doesn't put one's tent behind the rock outcroppings all around the area, one will be directly in the path of the night winds. In other words, it is much better to sleep under the stars on the kopje at this time of year.

I usually do a star talk as all my clients lie in their sleeping bags staring up at the seeming infinitude of stars in the Namibian night sky. As we climb up the steep side of the kopje, I decide to keep the star talk to a minimum. Everyone seems already to be quite tired and our talent show has lasted deep into the night. The next morning we are up at 6:00 a.m. to get on the road to our next destination, the seaside town of Swakopmund.

During my star talk, I have to shush Vic, Gina, and Connor, who I name "The Three Mushkateers" several times as do several others. They are busy filling cups with a bottle of whiskey they brought up to the top of the kopje. Usually drinking is kept under a modicum of control on these adult trips so no one can get hurt if they are indeed drunk, especially here at Spitzkoppe. They are already beyond a modicum of control. My shushing is followed directly by their giggling, a few minute of silence, and then some more drunken laughter and chatter. After about twenty minutes of this, I send them farther down the kopje so the rest of the people can enjoy the star talk. "Sorry, Mat," they say as they take their party a hundred yards down from where we are. We can still hear their drunken laughter, but we ignore them.

As I finish the star talk, I'm met with a couple people's light clapping and several people snoring. I survey the people and count them to make sure I know how many people are up here and how many back at the campsite. I find my usual spot, a pockmark in the smooth surface of the granite. It is about twelve feet long and four feet wide. It isn't quite as protected as the deep erosion area where my passengers are sleeping, but I'm happy with its solitude. The wind usually blows from the east during the evenings up here so I place my head facing east. Right above my head is a nice lip in the rock that forces the wind to miss my head and only hit the tips of my feet.

As I lay down, I can still hear the Mushkateers' drunken cackling. I check my watch. It is well past 11:00 p.m., and they still seem to be going strong. I tell myself to let them drink a few more minutes and then I'll tell them to quiet down. I stare at the stars and marvel at the sheer number of them. Every time I lie down in this spot I am amazed by the view. The stars are endless here, another one of Spitzkoppe's great treasures.

Fifteen minutes into my ruminating about the stars someone yells, "Shut the hell up already, you idiots!" More giggling comes from the Mushkateers. There will be no silencing them. I make the command decision to go and talk to them. I affix my headlamp and flick it on. I stand up and I almost lose my sleeping bag as the wind has picked up considerably. I flip my mat over and put my shoes on top of it. I slink over to them, two with cups affixed to their faces. Connor holds the bottle up and is supping directly from it.

"Come on, guys," I say. "You know we're all getting up early and people are trying to sleep. I can appreciate your big win Connor, but you guys can celebrate all you want when you get to Swakopmund tomorrow." Vic offers me a cup. "Come have a drink with us, Mat." I shake my head. "I can smell that from here. I'm pretty sure I'll die if I take a sip of that." Gina shrugs at that and grabs the bottle from Connor. She gives herself another shot. They are going to be suffering in a few hours if they aren't already. "If you're not going to sleep then I'll take you back near the campsite so you're not bothering anyone," I insist. "No, no," they say. "We're going to sleep. Sorry." I'm not convinced but head back to my mattress.

I can't say how much later it is, but I awaken. Connor's faint singing reaches my ears. I am genuinely angry but don't want to get up from the warmth of my sleeping bag. I lay there for several seconds and then realize the wind is *whizzing* just over my head and across my feet. I decide to flick my sleeping bag so that it will unfold to cover all of me again. I flick it up and *FWHUUUUP!* the wind *rips* my sleeping bag from my hand and shoots it down the kopje like a giant vacuum is sucking it down the hill. "*Holy s--t!*" I yell involuntarily and burst out laughing. I am astounded at how fast my sleeping bag is escaping down the hill like an insane magic carpet.

I slip my boots on, affix my headlamp, and race down the kopje. Gale force winds blow at my back. Running down the hill, I have to take even greater care to keep myself from tripping and becoming a missile. I finally catch up with my sleeping bag before it lands in the acacia trees at the bottom of the kopje. I trudge my way back plotting Connor's imminent demise. I place my sleeping bag with the rest of my stuff under the lip. I bend my head down and battle back toward the sound of Connor's not-so-melodious voice.

When I arrive, I realize the Mushkateers brought themselves right back to where I shooed them from, probably because even in their drunken stupor they felt they were too far away from the rest of the group. The only reason everyone hasn't woken up from Connor is that the wind is so loud it drowns him out completely. There is barely anything left of Vic and Gina. The whiskey has successfully delivered them past the point of caring and pain.

Connor, with all his talents in full flight, seems just raring to go. "Connor. What the hell, man!" I yell at him. He swivels his drunken head at me, his eyes going off in two different directions.

"Hey Mat! Wanna drink?" He proffers the bottle to me.

"I told you hours ago to shut up! Now go to sleep!" I say.

He looks past me. He cocks his head as if to understand what he's seeing nevermind what I'm saying. He raises his hand and points. "Um, wow, yer stooff's leavin'."

I turn to look behind me and my eyes shoot open. All of my paraphernalia is making a break for it down the hill.

My sleeping bag is flying through the air like a nocturnal pterodactyl, my pillows are rolling down the hill in different directions like fairy-toed convicts making a jailbreak, and my mattress looks like the magic carpet from *Aladdin*. "S--t!" I'm seeing red. Connor makes a movement that would be a jump to his feet if he weren't so inebriated and in his very altruistic way slurs, "Oh! Lemme help ya get thoshhh shings…"

I grit my teeth. "Sit down, my man. You're not going anywhere." I press him down.

"Ooookay." He acquiesces and *lies* down. I race away after my stuff, my curses flying from my mouth at the speed of sound plus seventy miles per hour.

I find my sleeping bag, mattress, and one pillow, two hundred yards at the bottom of the kopje. Again, I am grateful none of them ended up in the acacia trees as I would have had to spend the rest of the night disengaging them from the tree's multitude of thorns. I search the area for my other pillow. There is nothing but bushman's grass until Spitzkoppe's gargantuan looming darkness against the star-filled sky a mile away. My pillow could very well be halfway to Angola by now. I roll up my sleeping bag and mattress and stuff my pillow under my arm. I don't bother to hike back up. I'm going to sleep in the truck.

I hike back to the campsite bent at 45 degrees into the wind. Rounding the base of the kopje to our campsite, one thing becomes immediately and troublingly apparent. The wind between the kopjes where the campsite is situated is at least another twenty miles an hour stronger. As I come up the path through the waist high grass I can see the campsite is in utter chaos. Our fire's coals have been sent scattering in every direction, as if some demon was readying its way into our dimension by sending out its tiny minions to burn it a welcoming path. Nick and another passenger, Kathy, are frantically racing around the campsite stomping out the little fiery bits. It is a good idea. If the fire hits the grass with this wind, we might just succeed in charring the entirety of Spitzkoppe's campgrounds if not all of Namibia. I drop my paraphernalia and race to join the fun.

Kathy laughs as I approach her. She yells to be heard above the wind. "I was in my tent when I became aware of the fact that I was *moving*! The wind was actually *moving the tent* with me in it! I came out when I heard Nick stomping out the coals."

I look over at Nick and he smiles his huge grin of amusement at me. "Want to help us, Rafiki?" he says. I laugh. Nick is always there to save someone or something. "You betcha. Let's do this."

As I race from one bit of flame racing about the campsite according to bursts of wind I look to see if there are any tents still standing. The tents of those who chose to sleep on the top of the kopje have been blown to other locations between large boulders, completely flattened, and/or stuck like unkempt tree-houses in the surrounding acacia trees. I can't help but laugh at the absurdity of it all. *I've seen some wind here before but the granite gods must be seriously angry this night.*

We are almost done with the little demons when Victoria, her lovely, English, eighteen-year old face contorted in a mask of horror and disbelief, appears in front of me. The last time I saw her was when I had finished my star chat and she was sleeping soundly next to her cousin. By her new demeanor I think someone has been blown off a cliff. She is trying to catch her breath. "What is it, Victoria?" I implore.

"My tent! My tent!" she screams above the roaring wind. I shake my head at her. "It's, it's, it's *VANISHED*!" she shrieks. I struggle not to laugh. I fail. My guffaws would echo loudly off the granite walls around us if the gale-force winds didn't carry them away. I grab her on the arms to steady her. "It is not vanished." I yell to her, "It's *somewhere* around here. We just have to find it!"

I look around the campsite but to no avail. Aside from the tents blown over on people and their bags inside their tents, Victoria's tent is nowhere to be seen. Now I become curious. Obviously, I need to find the tent as we need it for future use. Judging by the way the wind is being blown through our small canyon area, her tent could be waiting in Swakopmund for us by now. I walk around the truck and head down the path heading west.

Fifty yards down the path I find Victoria's tent. It is *thirty feet* above us wedged between two huge boulders. It looks like a terrified manta ray trying to escape some unnamed predator. I can't stop laughing when she appears at my side. "What?" she asks. I point up above us at the escaped tent. "Oh, my Gawd!" she exclaims. "How are we gonna get it down?" she asks completely baffled.

I collect myself. "I'll get it."

I clamber up to the tent and yank on its metal frame until it dislodges from its hiding place. It falls to the ground and is immediately blown back into the side of the boulders. I hold it there a moment. "Victoria, where are the tent bag and your fly-sheet?" I ask seriously. I always tell the passengers to keep them in the tent in the odd event a *typhoon* appears from no where.

Her eyes shoot open like I just figured out she murdered someone. "*Ohmygawd!*" she screams with her hands over her face. "*GONE!*" The look on her face is so dramatic I can't help but burst out laughing again. As I laugh, my tears are streaked across my face by the howling wind. This whole thing is definitely worth the price of admission.

Victoria and I manage to drag the tent onto the path and behind the cab of the truck, which blocks the wind. "Happy here?" I ask. She nods at me sheepishly. "Sleep well," I offer, and step back into the gale. I nearly get blown off my feet. I go around the truck to see how Nick and Kathy are doing. I find them in the truck.

I join Nick on the front benches. Kathy is in the backseat. We are quiet for a few moments listening to the roaring of the wind. The truck rocks with the stronger gusts. "Do you think we're safe in here?" Kathy asks. I look at Nick across from me. Neither of us are sure. We both laugh. I think about the Mushkateers and their safety. Comatose and prostrate, I'm thinking their safety is assured. They're about the only ones who *will* sleep soundly and windlessly through this night, having vanished themselves.

ARUSHA

Highlander's is a beautiful campsite situated in the Cederburgs of South Africa. It is owned and was built by Sparky, a thirty-something Scottish/South-African and former overlanding guide. An unbelievably hospitable, friendly, and congenial guy, Sparky, lives at Highlander's with his wife, Hope, making their dream of a bed/breakfast/ campsite/vineyard a reality. Sparky and Hope decided to place Highlander's at the bottom of the valley where the farmers grow a number of things, most especially, the grapes for their wine-producing.

Although a very arid area, bordering on desert, the area has the Oliphant's River that is dammed for the valley's agriculture. Rising above the campsite is an escarpment from which the water comes to feed the river. Up on the rim of the escarpment sits an enormous wooden cross. Placed there decades ago, it holds eternal vigilance over the life and death of all who live in the valley below. It is the destination for my passengers and me if they want to do a hike before the evening wine tasting. In order to get up to the cross, a few obstacles must be navigated, namely the irrigation channels, several barbed-wire fences, and the highway, which snakes its way along the escarpment a half-mile up from Highlander's. All in all, it is a difficult hike with tremendous photographic reward if you make it to the top.

We arrive to Highlander's at 3:00 p.m., and it is ridiculously hot. We are greeted by Sparky's crazy, but very cute, thirty-five-pound bull terrier named "Arusha." Arusha is a year and a half old and well known by all we overlanders for her insatiable habit of chasing flashlight beams willy-nilly, worming her way into one's tent and refusing to leave, and, of course, accompanying everyone on the hike up to the cross. Arusha is doubly loved as she is the sister of her bigger and crazier brother, Mufassa II, who lives one campsite farther north at Fiddler's Creek on the Orange River. *His* nuttiness is not about chasing flashlights. Rather, his involves grabbing huge rocks too large for his head. He rolls them on the ground while whimpering and growling incessantly and eventually rolls them into the river. He then barks himself hoarse at his tragic loss.

As we jockey the truck for a perfect parking spot, Arusha jumps perilously close to the wheels. Nick, Mwai, and I have learned the best way to park the truck without running her over is simply pick her up into the truck until we have finished parking, so we do. We love her unerring enthusiasm to be a part of the guests visiting her in her lovely home but don't love her fearlessness of moving vehicles.

As it is impossible to be out hiking in the 110-degree heat, I let everyone cool off by the pool for an hour and a half before we brave the hike. The only takers are the hardcore athletes and exercise freaks like myself: Allie, a petite, muscular, Aussie nurse with a huge mane of blond hair and an unending need to be in motion; Allie's traveling companion, Carol, a forty-seven-year-old nurse as exercise-obsessed as Allie; Jacob, a sixty-five-year-old Danish millionaire who is mostly deaf and who said next to nothing most of the trip; Gray, another Aussie and ex-professional Aussie Rules player; and Pamela, a sixty-two-year-old Aussie who loves everything in nature and who never misses a moment to see all the flora and fauna

Africa has to offer. All are armed with water, their cameras, and the most important item to keep one's legs from becoming ground meat, long pants. Of course, it is only when Arusha sees us assembling for the hike does she come smiling over to us and wags her tail in excitement for the great adventure. We set off with Arusha leading us.

Everyone makes it across the bridge and under the first barbed-wire fence easily. We stop to look at a pencil euphorbia and its poisonous latex "blood" that Bushmen used to use as both a poison and a way to cure toothache. Arusha trots around us not understanding our delay. I have to stoop and pat her on the head to try and curb her enthusiasm. "Easy, you little knucklehead," I say to her, laughing. She jumps up to grab the plant from my hand. "That's not for you, Arusha!" I laugh. She barks and trots off.

"Is she going to climb all the way up there with us?" Pamela asks me.

"This is what Arusha will do: She will climb up and down all the places she can and then will wait for us to carry her all the places she can't. She's very confident in everybody's appreciation of her. She will, however, quite conscientiously wait for the last person to make it down before returning home. She's a good egg that way," I say.

Pamela smiles appreciatively at Arusha's tongue-lolling face. "What a good doggy," she says.

"She really is," I say and pat her on the head once again for emphasis. We follow Arusha across the arid expanse toward the second barbed-wire fence, which sits at the bottom of the rock-strewn hill leading up to the highway.

As always with the fence, I hold two of the wires open so everyone can crawl through. Allie, in her usual way of trailblazing ahead of everyone, whether we are hiking or going for a run, hops over the fence farther down from us. Arusha, always the protector, follows Allie through the fence instead of sticking with us. I watch as

Allie races to the rocky slope and begins climbing a much tougher part of the hill, Arusha right at her heels. "Careful up there, Allie!" I call to her. "The drivers on the highway are maniacs!"

She throws me a wave. "Got it!" and she scrambles up the slippery slope. Everyone gets through the fence and heads up the hill. Seeing that Pamela may struggle, I hang back with her. Pamela smiles at me, and I take her hand. I begin helping her up the rocky slope.

"Wait doggy! Don't go out there!" I hear Allie yell above us. I can't see her from where I am standing with Pamela. I open my mouth to yell up to Allie that her name is Arusha and to grab her until I get up there. I usually carry Arusha across the highway to ensure her safety. Pamela, however, slips, and I grab her hand, my advice dying on my tongue. As I steady Pamela, I hear the screeching of the brakes, the sickening thump of a car hitting a body. Allie yells, "No, no, no!"

"Arushaaaa!" I yell in response, and scramble madly up the rocks to the highway.

When I reach the top and the highway, Allie is standing transfixed at the roadside with her hands over her mouth. I scan the road and see Arusha's crumpled body in the middle of the highway fifty yards away. I burst into a run toward her motionless body, the scream involuntarily escaping my lips, "Noooooooooo!" When I get to Arusha, lying on her side, I bend down expecting to see blood everywhere. Aside from some hair missing from the points where the car hit her, I see no blood. Arusha, however, gasps for breath.

Aware that she may have a neck injury, I scoop my hands under her head and body, as I know I have to get her out of the middle of the road. I feel the blood as my hand slips under her head. As I lift her from the road, she groans. A large clump of blood falls from her mouth and I sob. I fight the tears as I carry her little body from the road. Her ribs have almost certainly pierced her lungs. I have no idea what to do for her and the tears start flowing.

I move my hands over her body as if I can cure her just by making those useless movements. The others run across the highway. Allie and Carol take one look and hear Arusha's labored breathing and Allie says, "She's got punctured lungs. F--k."

"Is there anything we can do?" I ask desperately. They shake their heads sadly and shrug.

I stand up and search around for something we can lay Arusha on to carry her back to camp. There is nothing. Jacob steps up to me and for a moment I think he has an answer to this horror. It takes me a full three seconds to actually understand his question. "You what!?! You want, *what*!" I ask absolutely incredulous.

"I just want to know what the best way for me to go up the mountain is from here." The others gape at him. I'm so shocked by the question I actually answer, "Well, um, you have to go down the other side here, through that fence, and…"

Allie interrupts me. "Why don't you just find your own way, Jacob! We have something a little more important to take care of here, you *A--HOLE*!" Jacob throws up his hands and backs off. I come back from the shock of his question.

"I'm running back to the camp to get Sparky! Please stay with Arusha!" The group nods. I race across the highway and down the rocky slope.

The race back to Highlander's is the fastest I've ever run three-quarters of a mile. It is also the longest distance I've ever run. I keep telling myself not to cry in front of Sparky, that Arusha will be all right. When I reach the gate to the property, I can barely breathe. I race down a hill to the house where everyone is gathered by the large patio and its small pool. As soon as I see Sparky on the patio preparing for the wine tasting, I burst into tears. My passengers look at me in horror. They only know me as the safari guide who catches scorpions, elephant whispers, and handles deadly snakes. They think the worst.

"What is it, Mat!" many yell, but I can't answer them. I bolt over to Sparky. I can't get the words out past my tears and breathlessness.

"I'm so sorry, my man!…I'm…so…sorry!"

"What is it, Mat!?!" he tries to be calm.

I can't say it.

"Is it Arusha!" he hisses through clenched teeth. I nod, unable to say it. "Is she dead?" he asks not wanting to know the answer. I shake my head no. I just can't find the words.

"She's been hit. She ran out into the highway before we could grab her. It's bad…"

He cuts me off. "I can't see her, Mat! I can't see her," he says imploring me.

I don't know what to say. I more than understand considering what I have already seen.

Sparky's next line brings me back to speech. "I won't be able to put her down, Mat. Please, you're going to have to do it."

His despair brings me back my strength. I put my hand on Sparky's shoulder and say as clearly as I can, "I'll do it if I have to, but we might be able to save her. How far is the vet from here?"

He shakes his head. "It's forty kilometers."

I know it is probably hopeless. "We have to try," I say as convincingly as possible.

Sparky runs to grab the keys to his truck. I avoid the eyes of the passengers, many of whom are crying. Sparky and I race over to his pickup truck. I can see by the look on Sparky's face that this may be the hardest thing he has ever had to do in his life. He peels out of the driveway and heads for the highway. We say nothing as we race down the road. I have never been more at a loss for words.

When we arrive at Arusha's crumpled body, Sparky sobs as he sees her. I bite back the tears. He stops the truck and races over to her with me in tow. Despite her enormous pain, Arusha struggles up to greet Sparky. The tears explode from my eyes, as I watch her try to lick his face with her blood-soaked tongue.

"Her ribs are broken and she seems more comfortable on her right side so pick her up without bending her," Allie says.

Sparky slides his arms under Arusha. I move forward to support her head. She can barely breathe as we carry her to the truck. I almost climb in when I remember the rest of the group. "You all can make it back all right?" They are troopers. They all nod vigorously.

"Go, Mat! We'll be fine! Good luck with her! Hope she makes it!" I nod in appreciation at them and clamber into the back with Allie, Carol, and Arusha.

Sparky races back toward the house dialing the vet on his cell. No one answers. We gently stroke Arusha and give her words of encouragement. Allie and Carol monitor her as best they can but I can tell by Arusha's increasingly labored breathing she isn't going to make it. With every breath, Arusha has to gasp and pull her head from the floor, her eyes bulging with the effort. The three of us exchange glances. As we pull into the garage, Arusha's bowels empty onto the carpet and blood oozes from her mouth. Arusha shudders and breathes her last breath. I gently touch her pupil to see if indeed she is gone. There is no response.

"She's gone, Sparky," I choke out. Sparky gets out of the vehicle. I stroke Arusha's head lovingly as the ladies open the back doors. The girls climb out and look at me sadly. I mouth a thank you at them. They walk away. Sparky appears in the doorway. He bends his head down to Arusha. He starts to sob. I lay a hand on his arm and cry with him.

Sparky goes into the house, and I search for something to wrap Arusha in. He shouldn't have to see Arusha the way she looks. I eventually go down to our truck and get my own bath towel as I cannot find anything else. I wrap Arusha up and try cleaning the rug in the back of the truck. Sparky appears at my shoulder. "It's okay, Mat. I'll get it later." I nod at him and point at Arusha's covered form. "You don't have to use your towel, Mat," he says.

"It's fine, Sparky. I'm so sorry."

He lays a hand on my shoulder. "It's not your fault, Mat," he says. "I know she would run out in the highway like that. Stupid dog."

I know he doesn't mean it. "Do you want me to bury her somewhere?" I offer.

"I'll do it," he says. "Thank you, Mat." He bends down and gently lifts the toweled bundle. He cradles her to him and walks from the garage.

I wait a few moments and walk out myself, feeling like I shouldn't see where he is taking her to her final resting spot. When I reach the garage edge I peer around its corner, hoping I won't see him. The image I see will stay with me the rest of my life. Sparky walks slowly up a path out beyond the guest rooms. His head and shoulders bend protectively, lovingly around Arusha's inert form. His whole body shakes with the grief we all should never have to grieve but inevitably do. They disappear from view beyond the pepper trees that line the property.

CHAPTER THREE

DANCES WITH WHATEVERS

DANCES WITH MONITORS

It is 8:00 in the morning on Lake Malawi. It is already too hot to sleep any longer in the tent. Last night when we arrived here at Chinteche Resort in the dark, I strategically placed my tent in the shade of a huge mango tree where I usually place it. My back window faces the vast blue expanse of Lake Malawi unlike everyone else's tent openings, which face the lake. I place my front door facing the two-hundred yards of green grass that is the overlander's part of the resort because it allows me to see my favorite things here at Chinteche: its dense populations of Nile monitor lizards. Of all the places along the route between Vic Falls, Zimbabwe, and Zanzibar, this is my favorite campsite because of the opportunity to see these huge lizards. All day long, they come from the vegetation at the edge of the campsite to feed off whatever they might find in the short grasses. Most people think I'm bonkers with my affection for them, but I can't help but love their scaly wonder.

I scan the property for signs of the lizards. It is certainly warm enough for them to be out and about. There are none out at the moment. I'll have to go check out the small dump they have out beyond the northern edge of the campsite after breakfast. They are almost always there.

I crawl from the tent and head toward the canvas shade under which Pete, our cook, has set up breakfast. I smile at the few passengers already awake, Pete, and Nick, our driver. "Jambo, Rafiki," Nick says in Swahili. "Jambo, Rafiki," I say back, smiling. I grab a coffee cup and sit with a couple of the passengers. Of course, I face out toward the grass of the campsite ever watchful for the lizards.

Not five minutes go by with us discussing our big plans for the day when Bella, an eighteen-year-old from England, who is horrified by the monitors she has already seen this morning, interrupts with, "Mat! *There it is!* There's that *thing* I saw this morning!" I stop in midsentence and turn my head to see the five-foot lizard moving cautiously from a group of bushes well within the confines of the grassy area. He is no more than thirty yards from us. I judge the distance. I know just how fast these creatures can be. I don't wait. I place my coffee on the ground and race from my seat. As I clear the tent I hear someone yell, "Where the hell is he going?"

As I bolt toward the monitor, he scrunches himself down in the grass. He is going to employ his cryptic coloration to ensure his undetection. Remaining perfectly still is usually these animals' first line of defense against predators. This is great for me as I beeline for him. If he took off immediately, I'd never catch him.

I am ten yards from the lizard when he decides that his remaining still is not going to work. I'm onto him and he knows it. He twists around and bolts for the tree line. I put on the turbo boost. I'm right on his tail as the tree line rapidly approaches. I know from previous experience that I won't be able to catch him anywhere except above the back legs where the tail meets the body or on the neck. A monitor this size can easily bite off a few digits.

At three yards from him, I realize if I don't dive, he is going to be gone. I dive, my body parallel to the ground. My hand stretches out and lands right on the mark above his back legs even as my body bounces off the grass. He is too strong, however. Without even bothering to turn and bite me, he wriggles his muscular body free and races into the surrounding foliage.

"Damn!" escapes my lips. I stand and brush the grass and dirt from my chest and legs. Cheering reaches me as I survey my grass-stained front. I look back at the tent, and the passengers are clapping. Tina, a forty-two-year-old passenger from Canada, shakes her head. "Nice grab, Steve Irwin."

I come back to my coffee beaming. Most are looking at me like I'm nuts.

"Why do you do that?" Tina asks. "They look like dinosaurs that could tear you to shreds."

I laugh. "Oh yeah. You can get it from their teeth, their claws, and their tail. You have to be very careful with those guys. A couple years ago a baby monitor no more than about a foot long bit off the fingernail on my left pointy finger," I say with a smile.

She shakes her head again. "Then why do you do it?" she asks.

"To be honest? I *love* them! I also want you guys to see that they aren't monsters. I realize it stresses them out a bit, but people should see these creatures up close to see they aren't freaks of nature out to kill them. Here in Africa it is a tragedy because people kill them believing every snake is a cobra and every lizard is a cobra with legs. I'll catch one later and you guys can see just how beautiful these lizards are." Nick and Pete smile by the fire and shake their heads. They know I am never going to change. I pick up my coffee and think how I can catch one so they can admire them up close.

After breakfast, I head toward the northernmost point of the four-star resort with Tina and Marilena, another Canadian passenger. Forty yards down the path from the reception area sits a twelve-by-twelve foot, bamboo-fenced, trash-holding area. Another thirty yards to the right is a huge compost pile. It is there that a monitor can almost always be found feeding on tasty morsels left over from the kitchen. When we reach the holding area, we stop and peer down the path. Sometimes it looks like a scene from Jurassic Park with the huge lizards all feeding within the compost pit. I'm psyched as it is no different today.

There are three monitors: two four-foot lizards and a *huge* one, one of the largest I've ever seen, at least six and a half feet long. It looks like a small Komodo dragon with which it is first cousins. Adrenaline jumps into my system as I think about catching him. I know I can't make any mistakes with one that size. He could probably kill me if he bit or scratched me in the right place like my neck or wrists. I hold my hand up for Tina and Marilena to stay where they are. They nod at me wide-eyed with awe and horror. I can see it in their eyes: *You can't seriously be considering catching that thing.* You bet I am. I slink along the path toward the pit, trying to stalk as closely as possible before I make my break for them.

I get to about twenty yards away and they stop rummaging. They look at me suspiciously, their long, forked tongues testing the air. I wait for a couple minutes but they don't return to eating. I make the immediate decision to race after them. When I am ten yards away, they bolt in different directions, their reptilian bodies snaking all over the place. I head for the biggest one.

Being such a heavy-bodied lizard, it is hard for the big one to get going. I am right on his tail after ten steps. He races straight toward the thick thorn bushes. Just as his body reaches the thicket of thorns, I nab him just above the back legs and base of the tail with my right hand. My left hand grabs halfway down the tail. He is too strong for me to stop my momentum. His weight and strength and my inertia carry me face-first into the thorn bushes. I am determined, however.

For a spilt second we are immobile. Fortunately for me again this morning, he is more interested in getting away than turning and biting me. He pulls with his huge claws in the leaves and dirt. In order to capture him I would have to move farther forward to get him behind the head. I am not willing, however, to go any farther into the already stinging thorns. I decide to let him be. I release him. Like buckshot, he disappears with a scattering of leaves into the undergrowth.

Tina comes over to me as I try to extricate myself from the thorns. The skin on my face actually stretches as the thorns hold onto it. One breaks off in my jawline. Laughing, Tina helps remove the thorns from my clothes and skin. "You're such a nut," she says.

I reach up to my face and pull the half-inch long, wickedly curved thorn from my jawline. Blood runs down my neck. Marilena stands back and shakes her head at me.

"I can't help it," I say with a smile. "I love those things."

As we return past the holding area, the gardener is there with a big grin on his face. "What you do wit dem when you get dem?" He asks me. I smile. I know it is absurd to most rural Africans when they see me catching lizards and snakes. It is beyond most of them why one would love such creatures let alone try to catch them. In some places, people have told me that I have special magical powers because I handle snakes and lizards without dying.

"I just want to show my clients how beautiful they are." He scrunches up his face with obvious reptile disdain. "You know you don't have to run after dem," he says.

"Oh, no?" I say sardonically. *They ain't coming to me that's for sure.*

"You know dey climb into here." He points at the holding area. "Dey go in under de fence and den eat in dere. You just go in dere and catch dem." He points to the tunneled earth below the door to the trash area. He unhinges the door and opens it. The smell that flows out is almost tangible. It is terrible but looks like a monitor's heavenly buffet. *I like the way this man operates.* I ponder it a moment and then decide a deal is at hand.

"I tell you what my friend," I say. "If you come and get me at the campsite when you know they are in there, I will pay you a dollar US." His eyes light up like torches. He loves that idea, as it is close to a third of his daily salary. So do I. I shake his hand and smile at him. "I'm Mat," I say.

He smiles broadly. "I am Mano," he says. "I come and get you dis afternoon," he adds without any equivocation.

"Until this afternoon then, my new friend," I say.

It is 3:30 p.m. to be exact when Mano shows up to deliver the news with not nearly the enthusiasm I am there to receive it. "Dey are dere. I put rocks under de door and dey are trapped inside now."

I jump up from my chair from where we were sitting and chatting. "Anyone want to see a Nile monitor?" I ask grinning hugely. Tina and Marilena, both having already been with me on tour for twenty-eight days and our adventure this morning, know that something interesting is going to happen in the next half hour. "Lead the way," I say to Mano and make sure I have his money for him.

When we reach the trash area, we can hear the huge lizards moving about inside. It is hard to tell whether they are aware of us or not. "How many are there?" I ask. He holds up his fingers. *Two.* "How big are they?" I ask. He shrugs. He doesn't know. *Great.* This could be a bit of a problem.

It is only twelve by twelve feet. If they are both as big as the thornbeast I just tried to wrangle, there is not going to be a whole lot of room for me to catch them. If one tries to bite me and I have to get out of the way, I might jump right into jaws or tail of the other lizard. I am quite certain that I do not want to get bitten or smacked by either of their tails. I have been hit in the face by a karate kick from a full-grown man that hurt less than when I caught the five-foot monitor on Amakhala. I smile at them. *No guts, no monitor.*

"Okay. I'm going in," I say. "Here." I hand Mano the dollar. "In case I don't come back." I smile at them. He takes it from me. "Please do me the favor of putting the rocks back under the door after I go in. I'll let you know when I'm coming out," I say. Mano nods at me. Nothing in the way he nods makes me believe he believes I am coming out.

I pull the rocks away from the hole beneath the door and unhinge it. Mano grabs the big rock and stands ready. In one quick motion I open the door, hop in, and slam it shut behind me. I immediately hop again to my right and into a corner.

As I land in a pile of stinky mush, the lizards go berserk. They both try to scale the garbage and the walls to no avail. They tumble back down. Fortunately, they don't get the idea in their pea-sized brains that a good defense is a good offense. One is about the same size as the one I caught on Amakhala at nearly five feet long. The other is the thornbeast. "Awesome!" I yell and they laugh on the other side.

Fortunately, the logistics of my tag-team monitor wrestling situation is happily made easier by the fact that the trash on my side of the trash area has been removed. All there is on the floor are two palettes with enough space under them to fit a very large monitor lizard. The little one stays along the wall fighting to scale the bamboo and find his way to safety. The big one dives into the trash and with a few waves of his massive claws digs his way into and then under the palette. With him out of the way it is safe for me to catch the *little* one.

I search among the peels, papers, coffee filters, and other refuse for anything that remotely resembles a bag or a cloth I can put over its eyes.

"Are you okay in there?" Tina calls out.

"It's awesome in here. You should join me!" I yell. "We got two of them and one is huge! You're gonna looove them!"

"Well, don't get anything bitten off," she says. I laugh at that. "Aha!" I exclaim as I find an old potato sack. *Perfect for catching large, ornery reptiles.*

I hold the sack in my left hand and flip lightly through the trash. I want to stress the lizards out as little as possible. As I dig, I realize the smaller one has dug its way to the bottom of the pile and has wedged itself between the wall and the palette. It squirms slightly as I pull the trash away from it. I place the sack over the lizard's head first. He stops moving immediately. I then proceed to scoop big piles of slimy trash and place it over to the other side and away from the monster hiding under the other palette. It is stinky, horrible business but worth every stinky second.

I pull the palette slightly away from the lizard and the wall. With the bag over its head, the lizard believes, if it believes at all, that it is covered and safe, like a baby playing peek-a-boo. I see where the tail sticks out the back and then I decide how to grab it. I press my left hand where I think his neck is and my right on the spot where the back legs meet the powerful tail. The lizard stiffens instantly but then immediately does what I expect him to do: *thanatosis* or *playing dead*. It makes this potentially agonizing process sooooo much easier. I lift him from the ground and call out, "Coming out with the little one! Please put the rock back right after I come out!"

Mano pulls the rock away and opens the door. I jump out with the lizard. Mano jumps away from me and shuts the door. He rolls the rock back into place. I place the hapless lizard on the ground and slowly pull the bag from its head and back. As the bag comes off its head, the lizard blows itself up and hisses. It is impressive and everyone steps back from us. "It's okay guys. I'm gonna let this one go and we'll look at the other one. "Watch out. He's coming through!"

Everybody wisely steps away even farther. It is not impossible for this lizard to mistake a human standing completely still for a tree and make an effort to scale him or her. I release the lizard and stand back. It lifts its head and considers its situation. *The coast is clear.* He bolts for it through the opening between people and disappears into the brush.

"Let me go get the other one. He's even more impressive." Mano and another gardener look at me with a mixture of awe and horror. People just *don't* touch these creatures. "Please put the rock back again," I say to him. He nods at me excitedly. He may be horrified but he is equally fascinated. I pick up the potato sack again.

He pulls the rock away, and I flip back inside the trash area. Fortunately, the thornbeast relaxes under the palette. I take a moment to look at his beautiful blue-yellow marbled skin and powerful claws. He is the biggest lizard by far that I have ever caught in my entire life and probably ever will. As nutty as I am, I know anything larger would be too powerful for me to control.

Looking at him beneath the palette gives me goosebumps. I know just being able to handle one of these creatures is a privilege of privileges. I also know I need to be extremely careful as well. If he decides to fight me once I pick him up, there will be nothing I will be able to do with him. He is unquestionably stronger, pound for pound than I am and his bite is much worse than mine.

I take the sack in my right hand and with my left grab the palette. I slowly lift the palette and see his body tense. I throw the sack across his huge head and lift the palette up and away. He doesn't move a muscle. I blow out my breath, not realizing I was holding it. I look down at his tail lying between my feet. I just can't get over how big it is. It is a real life dragon lying at my feet like a treasure from nature.

I again measure the distance between where his head is and where his tail meets his legs. I cannot grab him and immediately lift him up. I lay my hands firmly on the back of his neck and front shoulders, just as I grab the base of his tail. He stiffens and hisses angrily but doesn't fight me. "Open the door!" I shout.

The rock rolls away from under the door, and the door flies open. In one move I lift the monitor from the ground and stand up. I cannot risk him struggling so immediately take three steps out of the trash area and lay him gently on the ground. Once again everyone jumps back, only a little farther. "Oh, my gawwwd!" Tina says behind me. "It's *huge*!"

I laugh. It is *huge*. I slide my right hand up and press on its upper body as I remove the bag with my left hand. Just like the smaller lizard earlier, it puffs itself up and hisses loudly. Even I jump with the rancor with which it hisses. Mano looks like he needs a hug. We look at the massive lizard beneath my hands as it puffs itself up and hisses and repeats the process. "Don't be afraid," I say to them. "Come touch him. See that he isn't a monster." There are nothing but headshakes all around. "Come on. Just come around toward the back of him and feel his skin."

Tina tentatively comes around. She is the definition of hesitation but I give her credit for even trying. With its hissing, it sounds like it might have a nuclear explosion. Tina reaches down and touches the monitor. Like a child, she strokes the lizard's back, awed and scared. She even looks like a little kid. There is magic in this moment. "He's so, so *scaly*," she says like a fascinated child. She strokes him reverently even as he puffs himself up. I feel like crying, I am so filled with joy about this moment.

After two minutes, Tina stands up from the monitor and stares at the creature like she has just been given something magical. As far as I'm concerned, she has. "Anyone else?" Marilena shakes her head. Hell will be hosting the Winter Olympics before she is going to touch one of these. Mano and the other gardener step even farther back from me like I am going to hand the creature to them. Hussein

Bolt wouldn't be able to run as fast as those two would run if I tried to hand it to them. I can't help but snicker at that image.

"All right everyone, I'm going to let him go. Same thing. Watch yourselves." I lift my hands up from the monitor and stand back. Like an exact replica of the other, the huge lizard considers the possibility of freedom and takes it. He bolts for it. The only difference is that he decides to bolt right for Mano. Like a crazed ballet dancer, Mano raises his right leg and jumps away from the charging monitor. It looks like a move right out of *Swan Lake*.

I stifle my laugh as Mano runs behind the trash area and does the heebie-jeebie dance. My bet is that he will never find another monitor for another crazy muzungu, ever. One dollar will never be enough for this horror. I watch the blue-yellow skin and whipping tail disappear into the bushes.

I look over at Tina and Marilena and smile. They smile back at me. They may never have the same joy that I have holding such an amazing reptile, but I can see that they appreciate that I am thrilled. That, I suppose, is thrilling enough for them.

HEEBIE-JEEBIES WITH RAIN SPIDERS

"Not again," I say as I enter the bathroom and spot the hand-sized shadow on the inside of the shower curtain. This bathroom, like all bathrooms at Ulovane, my safari-guiding school smack in the middle of Amakhala Game Reserve, is a hut with one-half wall completely open, a shower, a toilet, and a sink. It is cleverly made of wood and thatch. I hang my towel on the hook next to the shower and look around the rest of the bathroom with a careful eye.

Whenever I enter the bathroom, I always scan the ceiling, walls, floor, and shower for any creature that may be lurking there. It isn't impossible for there to be a boomslang in the wood of the roof, scorpions scuttling across the floor, or a Cape cobra wrapped around the toilet bowl, all of which could very easily ruin your day if not your life. I happen to love this fact that these creatures and others might be joining me in the bathroom. The only time I don't love it is when I see one on the *inside* of the shower curtain. Call me crazy, but I like to shower in solitude without having to worry about scrubbing the back of a potentially lethal creature as well.

I scrutinize the dark shadow lurking on the inside of the shower curtain and try and determine if it is what I think it is, a big, female rain spider. I'm always hoping I will be lucky enough to encounter my first baboon spider, a spider most would refer to as a tarantula. This one's eight legs are long and lean and relatively hairless compared to the legs of a mygalomorph like the baboon spider. I am disappointed that it isn't a baboon spider, but am still pleased to see a spider this big. I hit the shower curtain lightly to make her run off the curtain.

Belying her massive size, she bolts away to a fold inside the curtain farther up. I tap behind her again, and she runs to the other side of the curtain for a different fold. I've played this game before. I spread the curtain as wide as I can so no folds are apparent. She has nowhere to hide. I tap a third time and she bolts for the wall, her eight legs flying across the wood. She streaks up the wall, crosses the ceiling, and stops at a point right above the door. No matter how many times I see it, I'm amazed and a little horrified that something this big, with this many legs, is able to move that fast.

I frown at her precarious position above the door. I know the other students will be coming in later, and I know most particularly dislike rain spiders. I can't promise my eight-legged friend that she will survive an encounter if she falls from the ceiling onto one of the other students coming into the bathroom. I'd hate to see her a squashed stain on the bathroom floor. I shine my flashlight at her and study her some more from a different angle.

Although a very large spider with huge chelicerae and fangs, they are harmless. It would hurt considerably if one was bitten as their fangs are large, but their venom is harmless to humans. She is light brown, with a beautiful yellowish and dark brown pattern on her cephalothorax or front segment. I can't help admire her and think of how these spiders make a nest for their eggs.

Using her enormously strong silk, she weaves a pouch sometimes the size of a tennis ball made from leaves and other debris around her eggs. She then attaches the pouch with several extra thick silk strands in a strategic place like the roof of the bathroom, above the door at the study lodge, or a tree branch. She then hangs on the side of it or nearby to guard the nest from potential threats. It is truly remarkable to see one of these nests, the mother stuck on the side of it, held by just a few strands and holding steadfast in violent wind. I admire her for a moment and decide after the shower I'll move her.

As I shower, I consider how best to remove her. If I leave her she will probably be at the mercy of the next bathroom-goer. Although I know everyone here is an animal lover, it is always amazing to me how people who love animals will still think of spiders, snakes, and scorpions as some other classification of creature deserving death at best. As I dry off, I decide to prod her from her spot using my flashlight as the gentle persuader.

I know I have to be careful with her, as a fall from roof height could very easily damage her abdomen. Although spiders, like all arthropods, have an exoskeleton, rain spiders' are quite fragile and are easily damaged. That is why one must be very careful handling the largest spiders, like bird-eating spiders, even though they look like they could pull the broom out of your hand after you've hit one.

I stand on my tiptoes and wave the flashlight at her. She doesn't move. I blow at her, but that doesn't work either. I decide if I lightly brush her that will do the trick. I grasp the very end of the flashlight so that I can reach her. I gingerly approach her with the instrument. At an inch away, she raises herself up from her flattened position on the ceiling. I hesitate, not wanting her to jump off and land on my face. If she does, despite my arachnophile tendencies, I will probably run shrieking like a three-year-old girl from the bathroom, without my towel. I do not want that to happen. She holds her position. I close the distance to her with the flashlight.

Much to my chagrin, she bolts down the flashlight, down my arm and shoulder, and stops in the middle of my back. Ice shoots through my veins. *Well, you solved that problem, didn't you, Mat?* I almost start screaming at the top of my lungs. I realize something very important about myself at that instant: I love spiders and scorpions but if I don't get this thing off the center of my back in the next ten seconds I'm going to freak completely out. I categorically do not like showering with hand-sized spiders and I like them taking up residence in the middle of my back when I'm naked even less.

I freeze for a moment and consider my options. I don't relish the idea of her running up my back and onto my head or my face if I prod her again from below. I don't want to squish her either, although it is quickly becoming an option, not only because I don't want to hurt her but also because I don't want her to bite me if I press her against me. That could be painful and spider bites can be particularly itchy. As I have had four shoulder surgeries from my tennis days, my ability to scratch my back, particularly at that spot, will be more than a little difficult. I decide pushing her down is my best option.

I bring the flashlight to my shoulder. I slide it down toward her. She scuttles down to above my left kidney leaving a trail of silk behind her. I shudder. I bring the light below her and inch it slowly toward her. As I approach her, I can feel her heavy body inch backward up my back toward my head. Apparently she will not be abandoning me for less thrilling locations. I consider pressing myself up against the wall but realize she may decide that she should definitely stay in a nook between my back and the wall or I will crush her. I'm stumped.

At this moment, I can't help but think of my father who is an admitted arachnophobe. He once, with a project of great courage in order to get himself over his fear of spiders, kept a tarantula in a terrarium in his office. Despite his abject revulsion, he cared for the spider for three months, feeding it crickets he scrounged up around the factory. Unfortunately, it died as a result of eating contaminated crickets after the exterminator sprayed his offices. His effort was hugely admirable, but I'm pretty sure if he were in my present situation, his hair would have turned white and he would have spontaneously combusted.

I poke at her above my kidney. She races to the middle of my back silk flowing out behind her. I try again from above. She finds my other kidney. I try using my hand. She goes back to the middle of my back. I think a whimper escapes me but I can't be sure. I half think to see if there is someone watching this for a candid camera show. We might be doing this dance all night. I try one more time to push her up from the middle of my back. She takes that opportunity to race up my back to my shoulder and stop there.

I slowly peer over at her sitting on my shoulder. She is a beauty. I'm pretty sure she isn't looking at me with the same admiration that I have looking into her beady, little eight eyes. I look at her dark fangs. If she jumps on my face I know I am going to start screaming. I watch her as she watches me watching her. I shift my shoulder a little to inspire her to move forward toward my chest. She will be a lot easier to handle if she decides my front is as comfortable as my back. She stays where she is.

I slide my hand up toward my shoulder. If I can get her to climb on my hand this will be perfect. I inch my fingers up toward my collarbone but she doesn't move. My fingers touch her long front legs and she lifts them. Some spiders "taste" with their legs and apparently I'm not delicious enough to clamber aboard. I put my fingers beneath the raised legs and slide them a millimeter forward. She doesn't like that at all. She takes off down my back, down the towel, and onto the floor. If she had done the super-spider move of down the towel and flipped into the underside of the towel, I unquestionably would have made my toweless dash through the campsite shrieking. She races in between the sticks of the wall.

I can still feel her webbing all over my back. I pull my towel off and rub my back. It is extremely strong and clings to the towel. I'll be washing it tomorrow. I wrap it around me web side out and step to the light. I look around the bathroom to see if there is any other critter control I need to tend to. I don't see anything. As I shut off the light, I'm wondering how many people will actually appreciate my effort let alone want to hear about it. Certainly not my dad.

WALTZES WITH BOOMSLANGS

"Mat! Mat! Come quick! I killed a cobra!" Dumile says in his usual exuberant way. I get that sinking feeling of certainty in my stomach that another innocent reptile has died for no reason. I try not to frown at Dumile. I know he, like most Africans who have to live among some of the world's deadliest snakes like Cape cobras, puff adders, and rinkhals, are pathological when it comes to their fear of snakes. *Every* snake is a venomous snake and should be killed immediately. I found trying to explain that a very low percentage of snakes are actually venomous and that they are helpful in keeping the rodent population down in their village behind Leeuwenbosch, the lodge where I am working, is futile. The only good snake to most Africans, and probably the majority of people worldwide, is a dead one.

"How long was he?" I ask. He holds his hands out. About three feet. "What color was he?" I query. Dumile scrunches up his face. If he did that in a court of law his testimony would certainly have been thrown out immediately. "I don't know. Black." I can see I'll need to see the snake for proper investigation of the murder. "Can you show me?" I ask as congenially as possible.

I follow him out to the dumpster beyond the kitchen and tool shed. He approaches the dumpster with trepidation, perhaps unsure if he did indeed kill the hapless reptile. He stops at three yards from the dumpster. "I picked it up with a piece of cloth and threw it in there, in the corner." I nod at him and steel myself to see the dead creature.

I lean over the edge of the dumpster and search the corners. Sure enough a dark gray, lifeless, serpentine length sticks out from under a piece of cloth. I reach down to pick it up and Dumile steps away. I shake my head as I pick up the snake and look at its tongue hanging sideways from his crushed head. It is a wolf snake. A perfectly *harmless* wolf snake. I bite my tongue, not wanting to say something in anger. I take a moment before I explain it is a harmless creature.

I run my finger over the upper jaw where fangs would be if it were a cobra. Dumile stares at me like I've just lost my marbles. I'm sure he expects me to drop dead on the spot. "This is a wolf snake, Dumile. It is totally harmless. In fact, it is a very helpful snake." I let that sink in.

"Can we make a deal, my friend? How about any time you see a snake and you show it to me I'll give you seven rand [one dollar]?" He nods vigorously.

"I just have to show you?" he asks skeptically.

"Yes. But you *cannot* kill it. If you kill it, the deal is off." He nods and smiles his brilliant, shiny smile. "I'm going to find *a lot* of snakes for you." As he dances away with the prospect of new fortunes, I sadly lay the deceased reptile in the dumpster. I sigh. Snakes near civilization don't have a prayer.

Four months later and at least seventy rand richer, Dumile bursts into the kitchen where I am just about to dig into my scrambled eggs after the morning game drive. "Mat, Mat, come quick! There's a boomslang in the outhouse, and they're going to kill it if you don't come." A wry smile tugs at my lips. Dumile has been right about two of the ten snakes even after I have lent him *Reptiles of Southern Africa*. I don't think he cares ultimately, as his financial reward is not based on proper identification.

"Boomslang, huh?" He is positive this time. "Boomslang. No question." I set down my eggs. "Well, let's go save a life, my friend." We set out from the kitchen back toward where the intruding reptile is on the brink of annihilation.

As we round the hill to the village I can see a good portion of the village is out en masse. They stand in a circle around the outhouse, no one within fifteen feet of it. I can't help but smile. Some people believe snakes have special powers and those who are not afraid of them and handle them have magical powers as well. Snakes are believed to be capable of just about anything including flying, especially boomslangs, whose name actually means "tree snake."

Some snakes, or course, like rinkhals and spitting cobras, are also capable of "shooting" venom. The mechanism for this are muscles along the jawline pushing venom down into the fang and out a tiny hole like a thumb on the mouth of a hose. In other words, one can never be too far from a snake. As I look at the faces, I'm pretty sure at least some of them are there to see the stupid safari guide get bitten and die rather than weave any magic.

As I approach the outhouse, I see Ouboet standing defiantly at the back of the outhouse. He is the head of Xhosa staff at Leewenbosch. He is a very practical, no-nonsense man with a great sense of humor for whom I have great respect. I smile at him, and he points to the right back post holding up the tin and wood structure.

"Boomslang," he says matter-of-factly. He points at a woman. "She was in there with it." I look over at her and she shakes her head and shudders. She is *heebie-jeebied out*. It must have scared the bejeezus out of her.

I smile compassionately at her. "Don't worry, I'll get it." She looks at me like I'm a lunatic.

I peer into the outhouse and allow my eyes to adjust to the shadows even as my nose will surely not adjust to the smell. I can't see why anything would want to spend more than a couple necessary seconds in it. My eyes catch movement in the right back corner as I stick my head all the way in the doorway. A foot of the snake's gray length juts out from the space between the pole and the tin. Her huge, round eye stares at me as she flicks her tongue in and out of her mouth trying to identify what I am. It is a beautiful female boomslang. Judging from the size of her head and thickness, she must be about four and a half feet long at the most.

I duck back out and the people behind me step back. "Yup. A boomslang. I am going to need a stick and a bag." They stare at me like I asked, "I need a coffin and a grave." Ouboet searches the ground and picks a good-sized one. He tosses it to me. He says something in Xhosa to a woman near him and she wanders off. I'm quite certain I'm the only one who doesn't think I'm going to beat it to death with the stick.

I lean into the outhouse and slowly raise the stick toward the snake. She recoils and crams her serpentine length behind the pole. Her not striking and choosing to retreat is a good sign in case I need to handle her. She hasn't yet gotten to the point of no return where attempting to handle her would be an impossibility. Some experts argue that ounce for ounce, boomslangs have the most highly toxic venom of any snake. It is a hemotoxic venom, which they inject into their victims with curved fangs situated at the back of their mouths. The venom destroys red blood cells and causes tissue damage. It is also an anticoagulant. If she bites me and no antivenom is administered, I may bleed out from every bodily orifice. The only good thing about the venom is that it is slow working and most die a day or two after they are bitten. *Plenty of time to get taken to the hospital.*

With most of her crammed between the pole and the tin, it is obvious there is no way I am going to be able to get her from this side, a fact for which I am very grateful due to the stench. I step out of the outhouse and look over at Ouboet. He stands there unperturbed, waiting for me to perhaps give him the sign to be the savior of his people by chopping the snake in half. He holds up a plastic bag for me. That'll work. I take it from him and approach the back of the outhouse.

I survey her scales through the small gap between the tin sheets. I won't be able to grab her without pulling the tin sheet away from the pole. That being said, I will have to grab her first, before pulling the sheet away as she will drop to the ground, which will surely aggravate her. "All right, Ouboet, this is what I'm gonna do, but I need your help if you're willing to do it." He nods at me. "I am going to grab her by the tail and let her get used to me. I will hold open this bag and then give you the signal to pull open the tin sheet here. She will fall out and I will drop her into the bag. That okay with you?" Ouboet shrugs as if to say, "It's your life."

He takes his hammer and puts the nail-remover side on the sheet. I put the stick in the crevice and coax her tail out from its coil around the pole. My heart immediately starts pumping overtime as I slide my hand forward toward her gray coils and drop the stick. Checking to see her head is not pointed toward me, I gingerly wrap my fingers around a coil toward the end of her tail. She feels cool and smooth in my hand. I can't help but smile as I feel her powerful muscles close around my hand. *I am holding a boomslang*, *one of the deadliest snakes in the world in the palm of my hand.*

I don't let myself get carried away. She wraps herself quite tightly around my hand as I imagine she does when poised in a tree. It is this type of strength that allows her to hang upside down in a tree as she inexorably eats her food. She adjusts herself in the darkness of the outhouse and flicks her tongue in and out. She knows something is about to happen, but I can see that my hand to her is nothing more than another tree branch. I ready the bag in my left hand at waist level and nod at Ouboet.

He places his foot against the tin sheet. He leans back and pulls with his hammer. With a loud creaking, the tin and nails pull from the pole. The snake rears up, as she is exposed to the sudden light. Her head then falls toward the ground and I lift my arm as far out away from me as I can. I pull the bag toward her to meet her head and realize with a horrible stab of fear that *this snake is almost two feet longer than I thought*. Her head is almost on the ground, way past the lip of the bag!

An audible gasp escapes the crowd of onlookers as she raises her head up to my waist level. She sways steadily in front of me at my waist and I watch her like she is the last thing I will ever see. I very slowly lower the bag to accommodate her extra length, lift my right arm with her attached, and raise myself on my tiptoes, all simultaneously. To anyone watching from a distance it would look like I was waltzing around with a very thick rope. She tests the air, tests the air, tests the air with flicks of her tongue. I am not breathing. I measure the distance with just my eyes. The snake's head comes into contact with the bag's lip.

She looks into the dark depth of the bag for a moment. Again she tests it with her tongue. The darkness seems better than the light. Agonizingly slow, she straightens herself into the bag, and I help guide her in with my right arm. As her tail end heads into the bag, I open my right hand. Her coil releases from my hand, and I feel her full weight drop to the bottom. I quickly close the top. I twist it quickly and tie it off. With a whoosh my breath escapes me. I take a small stick and punch several tiny holes near the top of the twist so she can breathe. It is done. I feel like I'm about to have a heart attack.

"*Bathroom is free*," I say to the crowd to cover my nerves. Several people clap, and I adjust my face to a semblance of a smile. Ouboet shakes his head and smiles at me. He knows I was lucky but is still impressed.

"What are you going to do with it?" Ouboet asks the million-dollar question. Everyone in the village is extremely interested in this question. I laugh at the expressions on everyone's faces.

"I'll take it across the highway and put it on Shamwari's side." There are a number of concerned looks and head shakes. Shamwari, the ultra-swank reserve across the highway, is only eight hundred yards away from where we stand. It is definitely *not* far enough for them. Death is about the only distance they would be comfortable with. *What if she comes back and now she's angry?* I know some of them are thinking.

"I'll take her," a voice says behind me. Mason appears next to me and extends his hand. He's a new guide at Leeuwenbosch who is working with Will, Amakhala's vet, at Will's new vet school Vets Gone Wild. "I'm going over to the school. I'll let her go over there." I hand him the bag.

"Thanks, dude." The crowd breathes a communal sigh of relief as the school is at least fifteen kilometers away. Mason walks over and puts it in the back of his pickup truck.

"That was cool," Mason says. "Not something I would've done, but cool."

I laugh. "Makes sure she finds a nice tree," I say and head back toward the lodge and my cold eggs.

Ten minutes later, I am finishing my cold eggs and about to eat my colder toast when Dumile bursts back into the kitchen. "Mat! Mat! It's out! It's out!" he screams like Chicken Little.

"How is that even possible?" I ask, completely exasperated.

"Someone opened the bag to see it, and it crawled out of the bag!" he responds.

I try to understand the logistics of it. It has been ten minutes since I parted company with her and Mason and he should be a good third of the way over to the other side of the reserve by now.

"Where is it?" I ask. He points out the window toward the opposite side of the lodge.

"At the main lodge."

"What the hell is it doing there?" I ask.

Dumile only shrugs.

"Whatever," I say. "Let's go catch her again. If I get bitten and die, I'm gonna kill somebody."

Dumile and I race over to the main house. Sure enough, the pickup truck is there with a crowd of workers around it. Beneath it, the snake is coiled up and hissing angrily at Ouboet who is busy trying to poke at the snake with a steel pole to coax it out from under the truck. I don't bother to ask what happened.

I grab another bag close by. I kneel on the ground next to the truck to survey the drama and make a game plan. Ouboet then presses the pole onto the irate serpent's neck just behind the head. The rear fangs are perfectly visible as she tries to bite the steel intruder just behind her neck. I hate to see her harassed like this. I decide to try again what worked minutes before. I lay the bag down in front of her face and open it. "When I say let go, Ouboet, let go. On three." He nods at me from the other side of the truck. "One. Two. Three!" He lifts the pole. The angry boomslang shoots forward into the bag, and I close the top. I spin the bag to disorient her and keep her in the bottom while I tie it off.

I stand up with as disappointed a look on my face as I can muster. "Should I take her myself?" I ask as I poke some tiny holes in the bag for her to breathe yet again. Mason shakes his head. "I'll take her. Sorry. Some of the guys wanted to see her and she was right at the opening when I untied it. Scared the s--t out of me! Won't happen again," he says sheepishly. I lay the snake in the back of the truck. "Thanks. I'm pretty sure she doesn't need any more aggravation. I know I don't."

We watch as Mason drives off. Dumile looks expectantly at me. "Does this mean I owe you for two snakes?" I ask.

"Sure," he says. I fish in my pocket for fourteen rand.

"You were right both times," I say.

"That's right," he says. "Boomslang, not a cobra, like I told you."

I smile at him. "Thanks for helping me save the same life…Twice."

CHAPTER FOUR

THE GIFT
OF SHARING
AFRICA

TOILET MONITOR

Everyone looks at me blankly as I stand over the 1 foot by 1 foot by 3 feet dimensions of our toilet in the Okavango Delta campsite. I can't help but take a queer pleasure in the variations of facial expressions written upon everyone's faces. It ranges from absolute incredulity to abject humor to unadulterated horror about the fact that we will all be squatting over this three-foot-square hole in the ground thirty yards out from the campsite to rid ourselves of our waste. There is always at least one, "I'm holding it till we get back." The amazing thing is that some actually do.

My eyes rest on Kelly, whose face is a mask of serious consternation. I know she is making the great debate in her head: "Can I do this? I can do this. Can I do this? I can't do this…"

"The process is very simple, guys, although it is amazing how hard some people make it. We will put this plastic bag on a tree branch where the path to the toilet area begins. You take the plastic bag within which will be the shovel that you will use to scoop dirt down onto your business after you've deposited it. If the plastic bag is not hanging on the designated tree branch it means someone is using the toilet. You *will not* use the shovel to shovel anything that did not make it strategically into the hole. Only dirt. When you are done with the shovel, please put it back in the bag and then return the bag to the aforementioned designated tree branch." I check their faces to see that this is sinking in, so to speak.

"*Please*, and I mean *please*, *do not* shovel your poop into the bag and hang it back up. That is categorically *not* what the bag and shovel is for." There is laughter, as some people don't believe that this has happened.

"Trust me. People are creative. Don't shovel your poop into the bag. "Any questions?" Most still look at the hole with incredulity. "Does anyone want to christen the toilet first?" I offer.

Everyone follows the bush-choked path back to the campsite except Kelly and her boyfriend Alex. "Um, Mat. Are there snakes here?" she asks.

I think about the endless snakes abounding in the wilds of the Delta. I'll only give her a list if requested. "Don't worry about snakes, Kelly. When they hear you coming, they will remove themselves. Just make sure you make a lot of noise when you come to the toilet. You can always bring Alex with you to scare them off. It may seem like BS, but snakes are much more scared of you than you are of them."

"If I see a snake out here, Mat, I'm going to die," she says matter-of-factly. I don't tell her the old line that seems to resonate all too well with the African universe: *That which you resist, persists*. Somehow it is always the people who are most afraid of things that get visited by them. "Don't worry, Kell, I'll be here for you if you see a snake."

"Um-hmm," she says unconvinced.

It is twenty-four hours later that I hear Kelly screaming. "*Ahhhhhh! Snake! Snake!*" She comes bolting from the path leading to the toilets, her unhooked belt rattling loudly as she holds onto her pants. Most people, sitting on stools, playing cards or sunbathing on their sleeping mats as we rest after our morning hike, jump up as she enters the campsite. She spies me across the campsite, hopefully not seeing how hard it is for me not to smile. "It was green! It was green!" she screams as if being green wasn't nearly as cool as Kermit once suggested. I stride over to her just to make sure she doesn't actually do what she threatened to do in the case of a herpetological encounter.

"Where is it?" I ask, trying to conceal my enthusiasm. She points back toward the toilet.

"I was squatting down, and it just came out of the bushes right near me. It scared me to death. Oh my God! It went right by me! I didn't even get to go!"

"How long was it and how thick?"

She shakes her head. "I don't know. I saw the scales and bolted! "Maybe five feet and thick as my wrist."

I frown. At that length and thickness, if it were actually green, the only snake that could be that big is a male boomslang, a snake I do not want around the campsite.

"Will you be all right to show me? I promise I won't let anything happen to you." She nods at me although the idea is quite clearly anathema to her being. "Great!" I yell, my enthusiasm getting the better of me. "You can follow me."

We walk down the path toward the toilet. It is no mystery to me that no one else has joined us, including Alex. I check my mental data bank for the possible other snakes that I know to be green. The problem with many people, especially adrenalized ones, is that they tend to be terrible witnesses when it comes to identifying reptiles and amphibians.

Most people seem to think that all lizards, snakes, and frogs are green when in fact very few actually are. There are really only two snakes that are green that worry me in Africa. The green mamba is one, which doesn't live in the Delta, and the aforementioned male Boomslang, the other, that does. The boomslang, however, is an arboreal serpent that rarely, if ever, comes down to the ground. If it was in fact green, most likely it was a bush snake that is completely harmless. If it wasn't actually green, it could be anything and that could be a problem. I want Kelly to actually feel comfortable coming to the toilet so I offer her this information. Rule out the two green venomous snakes, I reason, and she will have no fear of snakes at the toilet.

As we reach the tiny clearing within which the toilet hole sits I hold up my hand to stop her. I peer around the bushes into the toilet area. "Which way did it go?" Snakes are receptive to vibration more than hearing through their jaw and "inner ear." I'm quite certain that if her escape didn't scare it away completely, our approach would anyway. That doesn't mean, however, we can't track it.

She points toward a twelve-foot termite mound to our left that is capped with a series of vines. It quite humorously looks like a giant, green-headed Rastafarian.

"It went into the vines on the termite mound?" I query.

She nods, her eyes wide with trepidation. I step into the clearing and scrutinize the mound for any movement or the coils of a serpent. I only see the thick roots of the neighboring tree growing through and around the mound as well as the vines. I look to the very top of the mound and stop. Something doesn't look quite right. A root hangs down from the top of the mound where no root should be. Sparks of excitement alight in my chest as I realize it is a tail. "Awesome!" I exclaim.

I tiptoe quickly to the bottom of the mound and peer up at the tail. I'm having a hard time understanding it as the tail of a snake. "Is it the snake?" she quips. It is definitely not a snake. It is ventrally flattened, the kind of tail used for propelling a creature through water. It is a dull bluish-black with yellow flecks, perfect for camouflage among the branches of trees overhanging water. I know exactly what it is and a joy explodes inside me. "That's no snake! It's a monitor lizard! Ha! Ha!"

Kelly scrunches her face at me. Judging from my enthusiasm it is something she may, in fact, like *less* than a snake. "Is it poisonous?" she asks.

I laugh again as I scope out how I am going to be able to get up the side of the termite mound and catch the creature. "No, but if you get bit you're probably going to lose whatever it bites." I get the sense behind me; Kelly is eyeing me like I'm a complete madman.

I scrutinize the thick vine growing from the mound at the top right next to the unsuspecting reptile's tail. It is definitely thick enough to hold my weight. Whether it does or not will be the interesting part. I take four steps back from the mound, remove my sweatshirt, and ready myself for my leap up to the mound. I judge that I will need one big step/leap halfway up the mound with my right foot. I will grab the vine with my left hand, take another step with my left foot, and grab the lizard with my right hand just above where the tail meets his body. This will render his powerful tail useless and allow me to control him from whipping around and biting me. I figure I will then jump down with him to the ground, grab my sweatshirt, and cover his head. This usually causes these large lizards to go limp.

"What are you doing?" Kelly asks, as if it isn't obvious. "I'm going to catch him," I say. I don't look behind me but I'm certain her mouth is open and she is shaking her head. If this reptile proves to bite anything off my body, Kelly may never go out into the wilds of anywhere ever again. Certainly not with me.

One...Two...*Three*! I race for the mound and *leap*! My right foot hits the mound perfectly. My left hand grasps the vine perfectly. My left foot plants perfectly. My head, thirteen feet above the ground, rises up as if in slow motion at the monitor's level. As I feel suspended in space, my eyes widen with wonder at the lizard. It isn't just a monitor. It is a *rock monitor*, a species I've only seen one other time. I shoot my free hand forward and pin his back legs and tail to the mound. I immediately realize, however, that I cannot leap down with it.

The monitor spins his thick head around and attempts to bite me. Fortunately, the vine lies right next to my arm and he bites that. I realize, however, I have not quite thought this through. There is no way for me to hold him in my tenuous position. If I am going to catch him and not kill myself in the process I'll have to let go. With great reluctance I release the hapless lizard and hope he will stay and hold his ground here at the top of the mound. He doesn't.

Like a suicidal lemming, he jumps from the top of the mound, wriggling in the air, as if that would be enough to fly him through space. He lands perfectly at the bottom of the mound already in full sprint and heads, of course, *straight for Kelly*. She screams about as loud as any person I have ever heard scream.

I leap backward from the mound intent on pursuit hoping Kelly doesn't have a heart attack. The lizard is almost upon her when she bolts. I'm thanking the gods that be for that as a monitor's favorite haven from pursuit are trees. It is not impossible that had she stood completely still, the lizard would have used *her* for an escape tree. *Obviously not ideal for any of us.* I race after him as she exits her left toward the campsite. I grab my shirt as I go by it.

The lizard goes around a few small trees that will not support his bulky body. I am right on his tail, literally, slipping in the leaves on the ground. I try to grab him again as he cuts toward a big tree, but he wriggles free. He manages to make it to the trunk of a thick raintree. For whatever reason in his little reptilian brain, he stops four feet above the ground.

I eye him as he puffs himself up and hisses angrily at me. I slowly lift my jacket, admiring his display. He looks about twice as big all blown up. He hisses again, warning me. I shoot forward and cover his head and neck with the jacket while simultaneously grabbing him exactly there. He struggles, and there is a loud ripping sound as his claws catch in my jacket. I bring him to the ground and hold him only an instant before he goes completely limp.

I am ecstatic as I lift his subdued bulk from the ground. I can't wait to show everyone. I follow the path back toward the campsite with the prize in my arms, his tail hanging out of the jacket. It looks like I'm carrying a platter of brownies in my arms. I pass Devon, a two-meter-tall Canadian as I enter the campsite. He smiles at me and says "Hi," completely oblivious to the fact that my batch of brownies has an enormous tail sticking out the side of it. I laugh.

"You're going to want to see this," I say.

"See what?" he asks.

As I walk through the campsite, the Botswanan guides smile at my catch and shake their heads. They can't believe I am holding what I'm holding. Most reptiles to them are venomous and scary at *best*. Not wanting the lizard to be harmed if I release it within the campsite and not wanting anyone to freak out if it races toward them, I carry it to the edge of the water so that it will be able to make an easy escape away from everyone. "Come take a look at one of the Delta's treasures," I say to all relaxing in the campsite. Seeing the tail hanging out the bottom, they follow me to the edge of the water.

I slowly peel the jacket back from the thick lizard and hold him gently but firmly to the ground. When I remove the jacket from him, he stiffens but doesn't struggle. He knows it is better to remain still than to struggle at this point. After all, playing dead has seemed to work thus far. I haven't begun eating him. Everyone gathers around, and I explain how I found it sunbathing on the top of the termite mound.

The females of these lizards will actually use the termite mounds as an incubator for their eggs. They claw their way into the mound, lay their eggs, cover it loosely and allow the termites to do the rest. As the mounds are the perfect temperature within to incubate them, the mother lizard simply goes on her way, leaving the termite mound to do the rest.

I tell everyone to stand back as I am done showing off the beautiful lizard. I lift my hands from his head and slide back from him. He lifts his head slightly to see if indeed freedom is one sprint away. "Go on, buddy," I say and give him a little nudge on his tail. Like a rocket with legs, he shoots toward the bushes near the water. We all watch him go and I am filled with joy. "My first *rock* monitor," I say to myself. I turn to Kelly who is standing with Alex. "Sorry about that," I say to her.

She shakes her head. "You know that wasn't what I saw in the toilet," she says.

I laugh. "I wish I did see what you saw, but I'm very happy we saw what we did see. Do you want me to accompany you back to the toilet?" I ask. Kelly shakes her head. "I'm…holding it till I get back."

MUZUNGU IN THE MIST

As I watch my childhood friend, Brian, slip and slide down the rich, dark earth on this 45-degree hillside in Bwindi Impenetrable Forest, Uganda, I can't but help think of the conversation we had as teenagers when I was already a world traveler:

Brian: I want to go traveling with you but I'm scared of bugs. If I come you have to kill the bugs.

Me: They are not bugs. They are *insects* and I won't kill them.

Brian: Whatever. You'll take care of them though, right?

Me: Yes, but I'm not killing anything.

Brian: Fine. I'll go traveling with you just as long as you take care of the bugs.

Me: They're not bugs.

Brian: Whatever. Just don't let them get to me.

Me (not believing he'll go anywhere, ever): Fine.

Yet here he is, the *actual* Brian, my childhood friend who hates insects and exercise, refuses to admit that he has asthma, and who received the news with barely contained enthusiasm that it was indeed true the rangers would carry you to and from the gorillas if necessary.

Someone's juggling snowballs in Hell, I think as I watch him lift himself from the vegetation-choked ground, and yet, I am also filled with a huge sense of pride and warmth that my friend has come here to the Virunga Mountains looking for one of Africa's most cherished and endangered creatures, the Mountain Gorillas. It gives me hope for a moment: *If Brian has made it here, ANYONE can.*

I am further inspired by my sixty-eight-year-old, athletic, iron-willed father, Ken, on his second trip to Africa with me, and Brian's handsome, contemplative friend, Les. Les has never been outside the continental United States before, yet is now following his travel-blind buddy to this jaunt across Africa. As all my other clients on this overland trip from Nairobi have already come to the gorillas over the previous three days in the area, we are fortunate enough to do it as a foursome.

There are a potential eight permits given per gorilla family, per day. This means that only eight people are allowed to see a family group and only for one hour at a time. It is limited to one hour to ensure that the gorillas have minimal exposure to our communicable diseases since we share 98 percent of the same genetic material. When we are with them, we must stay nine yards away, if possible, to ensure their safety as well. The gorillas are allowed to approach us, although quite often the rangers will dissuade them by *tsk-tsking* them away. This day, although the other four permits were purchased, no one else materialized for our magical experience.

At the front of our line, Brian slips for the umpteenth time and our guide Okello decides to stop. He shoulders his AK-47, which he and some of his fellow rangers have to protect us from a number of possible but unlikely events such as running into poachers, elephants, buffalo, and even an angry rogue silverback gorilla. He helps Brian up from the ground. I can't help but snicker way at the back of our line. When Brian was young, he was a damn good swimmer. Anything that required legwork, however, was not his favorite. Watching him trek through the dense forest of Uganda is like watching a fleshy C-3PO tackle the slopes.

I try and hide my laughter by pretending I'm scanning for birds in the canopy. "It's okay, you can laugh," he says, looking up at me and my uncontained smile.

"Sorry, dude. I can't help it. It's like you're just learning to use your legs." He understands how funny it looks. The last time Brian did something cardiovascular was at the turn of the century, literally.

"You want to come up front with me so you can laugh even more?" he asks good-naturedly. I decline. If I laugh any harder, I might scare the gorillas away and they are close. Okello gestures for us to follow him.

After about another hundred yards down the steep incline we hear a whistle. It is the trackers. The rangers whistle back. The trackers are the ones who act not only as the locaters of the gorilla families but also as the antipoaching patrols. They also collect endless data on gorilla behavior within the habituated families. Each evening they mark where the gorillas are resting in their self-made nests. The following day they go out early to locate them again so that the visiting tourists can find them as quickly as possible. They are constantly in contact with the rangers via walkie-talkie so the rangers can guide the tourists through the protected forest. It is a fantastic process that works exceptionally well as one of the best, sustainable ecotourism systems in the world.

We cut across the hillside and head toward the sound of the first whistle. After thirty yards a strong odor assaults our nostrils. Those who do not know the smell would think their deodorant just stopped working and their armpits just picked up three weeks of stench. For those who know that gorillas give off an incredibly powerful smell from their apocrine glands, they know that they are near. Adrenaline jumps into my veins as I see a couple of the rangers crouch down and gesture back for us to follow them. For the second time in my life I'm about to see mountain gorillas. For Brian, my dad, and Les it will be their first. It is a dream coming true.

I am almost disappointed that we have found them already. It has only been twenty minutes since we left the ranger station. The last time I trekked the gorillas in the Congo, it took five hours to find them. The optimal is about two hours so that you get a good feel for the forests within which the gorillas live. For those who don't love trekking, no names being mentioned, twenty minutes is a blessing.

A massive roar reverberates through the hills around us and we jump. It is like King Kong himself might come crashing through the thick vegetation. We jerk our heads to find the source. Thirty yards to our left, sitting in a dense pocket of thistle, is a huge silverback, a mature male gorilla. I look at the expressions of fear and wonder on the faces of my father, Brian, and Les and smile. I can tell by that look they will never forget the sound of the world's largest primate. As scary as it is, it is a mythical, *magical* sound.

The rangers gather us together and move us from the path they have carved with their machetes. Although the silverback is to our left, we have not seen the blackback, a younger male who has not yet aged to the silvery-gray of maturity, to our right. He is no more than five yards from us, lazing in the deep shade of the foliage. He is entirely unconcerned by us and munches languorously on some leaves from a tree branch he has pulled down to his face. We start snapping photos of him as one of the rangers moves to within six feet of him to move an offending branch blocking our photo possibilities.

As we watch, I am once again astounded by our proximity to them. They have about as much interest in us as any other member of their family. I know it takes a year for the rangers to habituate them, a process that is not only arduous but potentially dangerous as well. The rangers introduce themselves to the gorilla family and allow for the reigning silverback to display ferociously and even charge them as the family flees willy-nilly into the surrounding vegetation, sometimes for miles. To the silverback, they behave submissively, which tends, at least, to keep the silverback from killing them. Each day they present themselves and will gain more and more trust from the gorillas until one day the family accepts their presence, and subsequently any humans' presence, as nothing particularly unusual in everyday life. Nothing unusual for them, *but a privilege of privileges for us.*

We are here for five minutes when the blackback decides to rouse himself from his nap place. Okello signals for us to stand back from the path and we bunch together three deep. I stand with my father just in front of me, Brian and Les to his left, and our other guide, Isaac, stands in front of my father. The ape crawls slowly from the bushes and casts us a momentary glance. It seems as long as we remain stationary he is going to pass by us by a few feet.

The blackback comes toward us on his knuckles. He slowly hunches by me and my father. He passes by Isaac and *WHAM!* Isaac falls back into my father. The blackback moves off with a couple quick steps and Isaac laughs, his white teeth bright in his beaming face. He rubs his shoulder absently and laughs. "He always does that! Ha ha! *Every* time he see me, he hit me. It is game we play."

I widen my eyes at that and am jealous for a moment that this man gets to have such an intimate relationship with this mythical creature. I'm also not so sure about the healthy prospect of future games with this gorilla when he becomes a four-hundred-pound silverback. I'm not sure gorillas know their own strength. I ask him as much.

"He never would hurt me. No. We are family." He smiles again and my worries for his future are assuaged. "Come. He is going back to the family. They are moving off farther down."

My father and Les move off with Okello and the trackers. Brian is having a bit of a time finding his feet so I stay with him. We head along the side of the hill toward where the rest of the group is heading as best as we can. Moving down the hill is much easier than moving across it and we both slip and slide as we go.

Isaac looks back at us and comes to retrieve us. "Come," he says. "We must keep up." Brian gives him an eyebrow raise, suggesting he's doing his best. Isaac flashes his pearly whites and nods. "Hakuna matata," he says and walks just in front of us, his machete ready to chop a new path if necessary.

We walk three hundred yards and Isaac stops. He points to a small copse of trees ten yards in front of us. Sitting at the base of them, in a state of seeming melancholia, is another blackback. We can no longer see or hear my father, Les, and the rest of the group. It is a nice feeling to have the gorilla to ourselves. "He not happy," says Isaac. I nod. He definitely looks like he is not happy.

"What's he grumpy about?" I ask. Isaac shrugs his shoulders. I guess getting the blues is a part of the shared 98 percent genetic material.

"We go around," Isaac says and points to a makeshift path up and around the copse of trees.

We clamber up the steep slope and keep an eye on the melancholy ape. I have to smile, as the gorilla appears to be practicing the art of looking without looking. He has stopped eating and has his big head cocked toward us, but refuses to look directly at us. It is comical. Watching the gorilla not watch us, we follow Isaac, Brian right in front of me.

We are fifteen yards above and left of "Grumpy" when Brian slips. He goes down awkwardly on his leg and hip. He slides momentarily until he halts his descent by grabbing onto some branches.

Grumpy snaps his head toward us and eyes us suspiciously. My heart stops in my chest. There's no way he's not going to charge. Isaac holds up his hand for Brian to wait a moment. None of us move. I can hear my heart beating in my chest. We stare at each other for a full minute. Satisfied that we aren't a threat, Grumpy turns his head slightly and goes back to his half-interested state.

We quickly help Brian to his feet and dust him off. Grumpy keeps his head cocked toward us but is obviously not interested in moving from his contemplative spot. We continue on the path keeping a watchful eye on him. As we reach the other side of the gorilla, he purposefully ignores us. I can't help but think he is acting like Brian used to when we were in high school and quarreling. "This way," Isaac says and heads straight and slightly down the hillside.

The trail we follow through the dense underbrush opens up at the top of a huge hill easily five hundred yards down and four hundred yards across. The whole hill is bereft of any big trees. A muddy game trail runs down the left side of it and, at a third of the way from the bottom, turns abruptly right. At the bottom right corner of the hill from our location is our group and the black dots in the foliage that is our gorilla family. I look down the 60-degree angle of the hill and realize, according to recent history, there is no way Brian is going to make it down the hill without falling on his butt at least once. Problem is, once will be enough for him to end up at the bottom of the hill, possibly muddy and broken in a couple dozen places. Apparently Isaac is thinking the same thing. "Maybe you hold onto me?" He suggests to Brian. I nod vigorously and Brian wisely agrees.

Brian sticks his arms out at right angles to himself and puts them on Isaac's shoulders. As Isaac adjusts himself to accommodate Brian's weight, something catches his peripheral vision. He holds up his hand and points to our left. As we look, I draw my breath in. My face lights up. Coming down a game trail that runs the length of the top of the hill are *two silverbacks*. They knuckle their way toward us with determined nonchalance, completely unbothered by our presence fifty yards in front of them. I turn to Brian with as big a grin as I have ever had in my life and bunch my fists in front of me. *Yes! Hugest score, ever!*

There is really nowhere for us to go. To our right is the impossibly steep side of the hill. Below us is the treacherous incline of the open hill. We obviously cannot stay on the path or they are going to knuckle their way over us on their way to wherever they may be going. Isaac gestures for us to sit on the hill with our hands behind us to keep us from sliding down onto the passing gorillas. "Keep your head down and don't look them in the eye," he says to us. Isaac and I put Brian just above and behind us so that we, who understand not to respond to the gorillas' proximity, particularly if they stop to check us out, are a meager first line of defense.

I am used to dangerous, African animals passing in close proximity to me although my heart still beats like thunder in my chest every time. I am hoping that Brian, however, is not as worried about them as I am for him. You never know what someone is going to do when faced with the ultimate in primordial vulnerability such as an encounter with two, four-hundred-pound silverbacks passing no more than five feet in front of you. If they stop to check you out for whatever reason, not everyone has the willpower to keep themselves from running away like a headless chicken and screaming, the worst thing one can do. I'm praying Brian is not one of them as we could not be more vulnerable at this moment. Brian asked me to deal with bugs not gorillas.

Twenty yards, fifteen yards, ten yards, they approach like creatures perfectly content with their dominion in paradise. One massive fist in front of the other, their rear-ends swinging behind them, it easy to see how they are the most powerful primate of all of us with *the strength of ten men*. They look around them, down the hill, at us ahead of them with complete seeming disinterest. I know, however, that if we were to do anything they didn't like, they would easily pull us apart like jerk chicken. One of them could do that. Two of them could pull us apart into enough pieces they wouldn't be able to put us back together with the right parts going to the right persons, ever.

Isaac gestures for Brian to lean farther back against the hill behind us. Isaac and I dig our feet into the dark earth. Our feet are no more than five feet from the path. If they decide to stop and inspect us, we are completely at their mercy. When they are five yards from us, I drop my head and slouch my shoulders. I can see their bulk with my peripheral vision and have to make a concentrated effort not to raise my head and look at these magnificent creatures. I am *bursting* with joy. I suck in my breath as the first one reaches me. Although it is daunting to be this close, I want to stretch out and touch his head and the silvery hairs on his back. I refrain.

His huge domed head, massive shoulders, thick fur, and comically smaller rear-end pass by with only a sidelong glace. His smell is palpable. Two seconds later, the second one enters into our arena just as uninterested. Like an exact duplicate he goes by as if we are invisible. What feels like forever really takes five seconds to happen. As we watch their silver backs and black butts continue on down the path from us, a rush of elation courses through me.

"*TWO SILVERBACKS not five feet from us*!" I hiss. I look at Brian, thankful that he behaved like a champ. "Dude! I could not have asked for a better experience for you! Ha ha!" I hold my hand for a high-five. He smacks it. "Amazing," he says, spellbound. "*Amazing*." Isaac smiles. He knows that was a privilege with a capital *P*.

After we are done congratulating ourselves, we look for the others below. We can still see the couple of black specks in the trees above the other specks that are my dad, Les, and the other trackers still at the bottom right of the hill. We focus on the hill. It occurs to me that the powers-that-be gave us the gorilla encounter because this hill might be the last thing we ever do. I quickly push the thought aside. *There's plenty of vegetation to slow our downward descent if we trip.*

Isaac looks at us. "Are we ready to go down?" We nod at him and he gestures for Brian to put his hands on his shoulders, which he does. Isaac starts down the hill, planting his feet sideways to keep himself from sliding. He nods for Brian to do the same. It is about as steep a hill I have ever attempted to go down, ever. I'm amazed the dirt actually stays on the hillside.

We take it very slowly. I'm sure it would be comical to watch our progress if there were someone actually around to monitor us. Isaac takes small, sideways steps with extreme care to ensure that he doesn't slip and end up with Brian's six-foot frame crumpled on top of him. Brian mirrors Isaac's steps, gingerly feeling the ground beneath him for stability. I follow close behind in case I need to grab Brian. I realize the silliness of it, of course. I picture it like in the cartoons. If Isaac slips, then Brian slips, and I grab Brian, we would then all go down the hill creating a giant mud ball with our legs and arms and a couple of thistle bushes sticking out.

We reach the turn in the path that will take us diagonally down and across the hill. *So far so good.* Isaac stops before he makes the turn. He looks at both of us to see if all is hunky-dory. It is until he turns and steps toward the diagonal path. Brian doesn't follow in unison. Brian's left hand finds space, and his body leans forward. Gravity does the rest.

Brian's right hand slips off Isaac's shoulder. His hands pinwheel in empty space. He steps forward to stop his momentum but only succeeds in beginning the inevitable face plant. I try to grab him but miss his hood, which is probably a good thing, as

I would have most assuredly snapped his neck. Brian goes face first down the hill. My hands shoot to my face, as I watch him roll down the thick foliage off the path below us. The waist-high shrubbery gives way with crackling and snapping as two, three, four times he rolls, gaining momentum, and then…*Fooomp*! Brian *disappears*.

"Holy S-----t!" escapes my lips. *My friend is dead. My friend just rolled down the side of this hill, fell off a cliff, and now he is dead and it's my fault*! Isaac and I slide the fifteen feet forward to the spot where Brian hit the lip of what I am praying is not a cliff. *Please don't be dead! Please don't be dead*! We both look down to see what has become of my childhood friend. Four feet below us, Brian lies in a clump of crushed thistle and other juicy vegetation. Brian struggles to gain his feet, which is practically impossible considering the angle of the hill. Quite involuntarily, I bust out laughing.

"It's not funny," he says, attempting to extricate himself from the clutches of several thistle bushes.

"Oh, my God, I thought you were dead!" I cackle. As Isaac and I bend to help him, I try and get myself under control. It's impossible. I can't stop laughing more from relief than comedy. Tears are running down my face.

"That was funny, huh?" he asks.

"Now that you're okay, I can say I wish I had that on film, my man!" I say. "Almost as good as the silverbacks. Priceless!"

He readjusts himself to regain some dignity. "Glad you enjoyed it." Isaac smiles at us and waits for Brian to latch back on.

"Are you okay?" Isaac asks.

"I will be," Brian responds. Brian reassumes his position attached to Isaac. "Isaac, no more sudden turns," Brian says.

Isaac smiles broadly. "No more falling down." We head diagonally across the hill to meet up with my father, Les, and the rest of the crew.

It is a wonderful sighting of the family. The silverback lies against a tree and watches with a lackadaisical interest as his family wanders and cavorts around him. Every now and then he gives himself a chest thumping that makes the rather preposterous sound of "*pok, pok, pok.*" One juvenile plays in the tree above us. Another has ascended thirty feet up into a tree twenty yards from us. One female sits on the ground plucking leaves from a thistle bush and occasionally looks over at us with a passing curiosity.

I am ecstatic that my father and my friends get to see the gorillas in this way. *Maximum reward with relative minimal effort.* We spend the rest of the fifteen minutes with them here in this green kingdom where peace and tranquility is rarely interrupted, thanks to these trackers, guides, rangers, and the government of Uganda. They, following in the footsteps of Diane Fossey in Rwanda, have done a tremendous amount to protect these creatures from those who would capture the babies for the illegal pet trade, kill the parents to make ashtrays from their hands or skulls, or those desiring to augment their diets with bushmeat. Okello tells us there will never be more than nine hundred of them as their territory has shrunk to the point where they have no where left to go. Any more than nine hundred and they will kill each other for territory. When Okello gestures for us to go, it is hard to leave them.

"We have to go back up that hill?" Brian asks with marked skepticism.

"I'll hold onto you to make sure you don't fall off any more cliffs," I say.

"Maybe they can carry me," he says half-joking. He knows that they will indeed carry him if it is necessary. Being handicapped or challenged does not exclude anyone from seeing the gorillas.

I'm hoping Brian will do it on his own. ""Let's see how far you get before they have to drag your butt up these hills."

My dad and Les fight up the incredibly steep hills like champs. Brian combats his asthma and the hills like a greater champ, as they seem to get steeper and steeper the higher we climb. Okello and Isaac assure Brian that they will carry him if he'd like them to, but he declines despite his laborious breathing. It takes us an hour and a half to reach the road back to the ranger station. Twenty minutes in, an hour and a half out. Not bad at all.

Walking down the road, I look over at my insect-fearing, exercise-hating, asthmatic, childhood friend who has conquered the Virunga Mountains like a true champion. I am filled with a profound pride that he has also conquered his fears and his limitations to have the privilege of a lifetime in seeing the Mountain Gorillas. I won't ever tell him this, but after his effort, if he does call an insect a bug, I'll reserve him that right.

NOT YOUR AVERAGE CAT

The lioness watches us roll our four, extended-bodied, Toyota Landcruisers to a stop, one hundred yards across the hippo pool with an intensity that makes me uncomfortable. She lies basking her pregnant belly on the top of what was once a termite mound, but it has long since worn away with the coming and going of the hippos in this dam. It is immediately evident she is a part of a conservation effort here in the park as she wears a collar around her tawny neck. The Serengeti has innumerable scientific and conservation-based efforts going on at any time and she is a part of one. One of the best ways to understand how an ecosystem is functioning is to understand what and how the apex predators like this female and her pride are doing. They must be particularly interested in this female as she is ready to give birth.

A stream trickles from the hippo pool down across a thirty-yard concrete road made to help spirit tourists across the stream when the Seronera River is high. We park perpendicularly to the road to get some photos of the hippos before we roll around to our right to get closer to her. From our vantage point, standing on our seats with our heads and shoulders through the rooftop, we can see everything around us 360 degrees. It is a magnificent spot for photos, particularly with the magnificent lioness right out in the open. No one in the world should miss this vista. *Except Bruce*. He is *hopefully* going to miss this and a lot more until I can get him back to Arusha and the hospital.

I look down at Bruce, a forty-four year old builder from the Australian outback, snoring, unconscious on the seat between his daughter, Eve, and myself. In a normal situation I would wake him up. Unfortunately, his situation is not normal. In fact, his situation is *off-the-charts* not normal. He is suffering from a complete, psychotic breakdown from his Larium, or antimalaria drug, and has been a raving maniac for the past twelve hours. (See *THIS IS AFRICA: True Tales of a Safari Guide's Lariam Days* for the complete story.) He has finally worn himself out and we can safely get back, at least for the moment, to doing what we came for: *Game viewing in the Serengeti.*

I look back to the lioness with my binoculars and I jump. She is staring right back at me. I pull the binos from my face and look at her posture. Her head is up like she is ready for predatory action. There is tension in her front legs. She is getting ready to move without question. However, there is also hesitation in her. I feel like I'm somewhere looking at the most beautiful woman in the room and thinking she can't be looking at me but absolutely looks like she is. It occurs to me to look behind me to see if there's a clock behind my head.

Behind me is the dirt road that slopes gently upward to the grasses. I peer into the depths of the waving grasses and get my *Aha!* moment. In the long grass stands a large male warthog wanting to venture down to the water to drink. He is a water-dependent species and will go down to water all day long even at the hottest parts of the day. Warthogs don't, however, relish the idea of wandering away from the safety of the long grasses and out into the open to do it. I say as much to the group.

I can see that he, too, knows that she is there. There is no way for her to catch him at this distance and he knows it. What I know he also knows is that for him to get to the water, he has to go along the left side of our vehicles, which means he will lose sight of the lioness if he does. He cannot risk that. *Better to be thirsty than dead.*

We watch this African standoff for a few minutes, almost hoping for the warthog to take the chance, not necessarily to see a kill, but at least to see her get up and make an effort to catch him. Well, some might want to see a kill if not the majority. I am one of those who does not love the idea although I would like to experience it just to be able to say I saw one. It *is* one of the most spectacular occurrences in nature. It is a part of the circle of life and, after all, one of the first questions I always get as a safari guide is how many kills I've seen. It's almost unprofessional to say I haven't seen any. After three years of guiding, I have yet to see one.

"Look, look, look!" says Gail, a thirty-four-year-old American in our vehicle with her sixty-seven-year-old dad, Jerry. She points with one hand and expertly holds her camera in the other clicking continuously. The lioness is crouched and eyeing something to our left. I look where she is looking and my blood turns to ice. Two baby Thompson's gazelles have pranced their way down to the water from the bushes. Too young to know better, they have simply found their way down to the stream's edge. Their mothers, not ten yards from them, are barely visible in the cover of the bushes where they are ruminating.

I am astounded at what the lioness does next. Instead of shooting straight toward them, she slinks down into a muddy area that will not permit a line of sight for the gazelles. It allows her to stalk to its end where she is then parallel to our vehicle. She immediately turns so she is perpendicular to us and slinks toward us with a grim determination. I know exactly what she is doing and I am amazed. She stalks toward us from twenty yards out. She is going to T-bone our car.

"Oh, my God! Oh, my God!" Mary, a thirty-eight-year-old surgeon from New Zealand cries from her seat. "She's coming right for me! What do I do? What do I do?" I try hard not to laugh. They are the exact words I said to myself when I was charged by our pride male, Mufasa, at Amakhala.

"Just stay calm and quiet and don't make any sudden moves. Lions quite often will lie right under the window of the car if there is shade there for it. It doesn't even know you're there. Go ahead and take your photos, Mary," I say. As the lioness crouches toward Mary, watching the gazelles *under* our vehicle, I think back to Mufasa's charge:

I had taken my insistent guests from Leeuwenbosch Lodge on Amakhala to the lion area against my better judgment. Usually it was mandatory for us to take them, as lions are the most iconic animals in Africa and nearly everyone's number one must-see. The only problem with that particular day was that Will, our resident veterinarian, had taken Scar, our female, from the area to put a prophylactic in her so she wouldn't breed anymore. I knew Mufasa was going to be looking for her, not in any mood to be appreciated, and the cubs would most certainly be hidden away where we would never find them.

We found Mufasa in all his massive, muscular glory padding angrily up and across a hill to find high ground to find his ladylove. I had to offroad to follow him so all could get a decent photo of something better than his rear-end. After about five minutes I could see he was not made happier by our presence and decided to leave him. Most lions sleep up to twenty hours a day and to get photos of a specimen like Mufasa, his huge muscles rippling beneath his golden hide as he stalks his territory, was a huge privilege. Everyone agreed it was better to leave him alone.

I descended the hill to the road and stopped the vehicle in a particularly beautiful spot to tell my clients about the dire situation lions face in Africa, having lost 90 percent of their numbers in the past sixty years. I sat up on the edge of the roofless Land Rover so I could comfortably look at them. After a minute, I decided to remove my sweater, as I was heating up. I lifted the sweater up to my head and struggled to get my arms out. It was then I heard a client scream, "He's coming! The lion is coming!" Although I wanted to freeze, I knew he would take me out as soon as he reached me. These people would get the great benefit on their vacation of watching their safari guide knocked forty-five miles an hour out of his vehicle by a five-hundred-pound lion into 270 pieces that the lion promptly ate. *Probably not a good idea to let that happen.*

I ripped the sweater over my head and threw it in the seat. I whipped around and saw Mufasa not sixty yards up the hill above us, charging straight for me. He was at full charging speed of forty-five miles an hour. I thought, *Oh, my God! Oh, my God! What do I do?* Well, thanks to training, I knew what to do. First and foremost, when a lion is charging, *stare into the lion's eyes.* I locked my eyes with his. I dropped into my seat and yelled to the clients, "Don't move!"

When Mufasa hit thirty yards, I raised my hand with everyone screaming and ducking behind me. He was something *awesome* to behold—a full-grown male lion in full charge with full intent to kill me. I smashed my hand, *BOOM!* against the vehicle's door with every ounce of adrenalized strength possible. Mufasa flinched and then turned his charge at the very last second. He barely skirted around the front of the vehicle and shot down the hill below us.

Unlike Mufasa, the lioness reaches the side of our car, two feet below Mary's camera. She slinks along its side toward the front. She moves directly up to the cruiser in front of us. Her ears are laid back as she peers around the front of the vehicle at her prey. I steal a glance over at the gazelles drinking from the stream. They are oblivious to her presence. I am amazed at her ingenuity. It took her exactly one second to make the decision to use the vehicles as cover for her charge. She hesitates, watching them.

Usually a lion cannot catch a Tommie unless she somehow manages to stalk right up next to one. A Tommie's top speed of fifty-five miles an hour is far faster than a lion, which is why cheetah are about the only predator that makes a habit of chasing them. In this case, however, our lioness has managed to close the gap between the impossible and possible by using our vehicles. She is only twenty yards from them at most. She waits for them to dip their heads back down to the water a final time. She bolts for them, a golden tornado of death.

The gazelles have enough time to look up before she is on them. A cry goes up from our vehicles. One gazelle shoots off toward the mothers. The other makes it ten feet before the lioness's jaws close around its neck. The lioness jerks her head once sideways and snaps the neck of the baby gazelle. Mercifully, it is over in a second. She stands in the cloud of dust she raised with her charge for a moment, waiting for the death twitching of the gazelle to subside. A minute later, she takes the lifeless gazelle and settles in the shade of an acacia to enjoy the spoils of her ingenious labor.

Although it is exciting to have seen the circle of life in action on this apex level, I am blessedly pleased I didn't have to hear the baby's cries like so many other animals do when they are not killed outright. I take solace in the taking of its young life that the lioness is most assuredly feeding herself to create milk to feed her own babies that are soon to join our world. Everyone is quiet as we pull away.

Bruce, awakened by the cry when the lioness bolted for the gazelles, stands up between his daughter and me. "What is it?" he asks. I am disappointed he is once again conscious, although a small part of me is interested to see what he will next have to say. I think about what I should tell him. Many people come to Africa just to witness what we just witnessed. If he were his normal self, he would probably be really displeased he missed the event. I decide to take the easy way out. "Ah, nothing you haven't seen, my man. Just a couple of gazelle, a lioness, and some hippos…"

ROGER, GERRY, AND ME

"Get the book, Mat!" Gerry hisses to me from the door of the ATP supervisor's office. I look up from his desk where I am packing away my things in my backpack. It has been a long, amazing day at the BNP Paribas Tennis Open, Indian Wells.

I look at him, a why? writ across my features.

"It's *Roger*! He's right *here*! Get your book!"

I almost ask, "Roger, *who*?" as my brain can't quite wrap around the concept that Gerry is talking about the one person in *human history* I'd most like to meet: *Roger Federer*. I am an antelope in the headlights. I've thought about meeting, if not playing, Roger Federer since I first saw him beat Andre Agassi in the Masters finals in 2003, 6-0 in one of the sets. I thought then he was the most ingenious tennis player I had ever seen and probably would ever see. *A magician with a tennis racquet. Now a tennis deity…*

I shove my backpack aside and search Gerry's desk for the brown paper bag with my book in it, which I had given to him to give to Roger. We had spent the last hour sifting through Gerry's unbelievable collection of African photos on his computer, which he had taken since the last time I had seen him on Amakhala Game Reserve six years ago. I find the book on the floor next to his bag. I grab it thinking, *Can this really be happening? He's gotta be kidding.*

Do I even really want to be meeting Roger Federer? As my hand closes on my book, I'm more than a little confident I want to meet Roger Federer. I jump up and race for the door.

As I get to the door I stop to comport myself. I take a deep breath and tell myself, *He's just another human being...He's just another human being*, a statement that has very little to no truth in it. I round the corner of the office and stop. Roger stands facing Gerry in his red-and-blue striped jumper talking to him as he has done ten thousand times over the past ten years. My face breaks into a grin that would probably kill the Cheshire Cat. I take my first step toward Roger Federer and tell myself, *Don't you dare throw up on him...*

SIX YEARS EARLIER

I'm sitting at the head of the table on the porch of our lodge at my safari guiding school, Ulovane Environmental Training. I'm outside because I don't want my studies to be interrupted by the six-week students having class inside the lodge. I am studying for my Level 2 test. Coming back to Ulovane for a week's break from our respective lodges to study is something all of us in the year program have done now for the past six months. It is coming down to the wire for me to say the least.

I have a month left of school and still have yet to pass the rifle test, the Level 2 test, and of course, the Trail's Guide test, which in itself requires me to pass the rifle test, the written test, and doing my VDPA or Viewing Potentially Dangerous Animals. I am more than a little stressed as I feel like I will have failed everything if I don't qualify for Trail's Guide. Trail's Guide will allow me to walk people through the wilds of Africa. Walking people through the wilds of Africa is what I most desire to do. *That IS the dream like playing professional tennis was once the dream.*

Matt Ford-Armstrong, seventeen, strides his long, lanky frame out onto the porch and smiles at me. He asks with his fine English accent if he can sit at the table with me. "Sure," I say, and bury my head back in my book. I don't want to enter into conversation at the moment and many of the new students can't help but ask a million questions about the program and what we have experienced being here. He sits down and says, "Hey, my dad's here. You should meet him." I nod at him and give him another unenthusiastic "Sure."

He had told me a month before when he had first come to Amakhala that his father worked on the Association of Tennis Professionals tour. This was in response to my having told him I had been a professional tennis player in my previous life. Having played the minor leagues, I never actually was on the ATP tour, a source of some not small psychic agony for me. Any further conversation about it wasn't going to be a winner between us. I didn't pursue it and neither did he. We did however talk a lot about our love of nature, something that transcends any age group.

As his father walks out onto the porch wearing big sunglasses and a wide-brimmed hat, I decide I'll just give a quick hello and go back to the tent to study if everybody wants to start talking. His father arrives at the table, points at the chair to my left, and in his pleasant English accent says, "May I sit heah?" I jab my pen toward the seat and say. "Please." I extend my hand and shake his. I steel myself for some small talk with Matt's dad and lean back in my chair as he sits down.

"It's lovely heah," he says, peering out over the porch out at Woodbury Plains where several herds of antelope, zebra, and other beasties can be seen grazing. I nod in agreement without looking at him. He could be anyone under those sunglasses and hat.

"Mat used to play professional tennis, Dad," Matt says.

"Really, have we met before?" Gerry asks, as he reaches for his sunglasses and hat to pull them from his head. Before I can answer with a "Probably not, I was mostly on the ITF circuit." Gerry finishes the disrobing of his head by taking off his hat, his thinning blond hair falling into place on a head that I had seen two hundred times before on TV if not more.

"*HOLY S--T!!! YOU'RE GERRY ARMSTRONG!*" I scream. "YOU'RE *GERRY,* ARMSTRONG!" I scream again in case he missed the first time.

He smiles at me. "Well, yes, I am."

Matt is surprised by my reaction. "You know him?" he asks.

"Do I *know* him?" I froth. "Do you have any idea how many times I pictured myself as a kid arguing with him at Center Court Wimbledon? Ha ha! Your dad is an absolute icon in my mind! He is a living legend! A living legend!"

Gerry laughs more from being uncomfortable than anything else. I continue to embarrass myself. "I saw the match where you threw McEnroe out of the Australian Open in 1990! Ha ha! That was *awesome!*" Gerry chuckles at this recognition of this well-known moment in tennis history. "I mean, Matt, told me that his dad worked on the ATP tour but I didn't put Armstrong together with *Armstrong!*" Gerry smiles good-naturedly at me and extends his hand again. "Well, it is very nice to meet you, Mat," he says.

We then spend the next two hours talking about life on the ATP Tour that I didn't get to live and my questions do not cease. I forget that I wasn't going to chat with anyone and go back to my tent. I'm almost annoying myself with all the details that I'm asking for, which Gerry is congenially providing me. Fortunately, he is as interested in life at Amakhala and how a tennis player became a safari guide as I am about his legendary life as the number one umpire and now supervisor of the ATP tour. We have an instant bond that I am more than pleased with.

Although I am very busy with studying, I take a break every chance I get to chat with Gerry. Gerry, on a break from the tour for a few days to see what his son is up to, is there to enjoy the reserve. Janice and Pieter, who own Ulovane, have been kind enough to include Gerry in the activities, the walks, the drives, the studies, and everything they are doing. He loves it. He has become, like me and so many others who come to Africa, what the French refer to as a "*Tet-Afrique*" or "Africa head."

Later in the day, Gerry comes back from one walk shaken yet excited. "I almost stepped on a puff adder!" he says. I truly appreciate his enthusiasm for this event. Most people would usually be calling the airlines to shorten their vacation.

"What happened?" I ask, just as excited.

"Well they were walking and everyone passed the snake and then the creature decided when I reached it that it had had enough and decide to let me know it was bothered! It hissed at me." I laugh. I had only seen one puff adder my entire time on the reserve. "Count yourself one of the lucky ones, Gerry!" I laugh.

"I do! I do!" he says enthusiastically.

He is a guy who really gets the wonder of Africa.

"I'm bummed I have to leave tomorrow," he adds.

I'm bummed he has to leave tomorrow as well, but I can't spend too much time grieving as the next day is my last chance to pass the rifle test, as I had failed it, quite unhappily yet again, this morning. If I don't pass my test, I feel that all I have worked for will be for nothing. Gerry and I say our goodbyes that evening and exchange our info to keep in touch. I am extraordinarily pleased I have met one of my childhood's icons and that he turned out to be such a great fellow.

The next day, in the early morning, I pass my rifle test. I am elated beyond elation. I had failed it three times and was terrified that I wouldn't be able to do it. I count it one of my greatest successes to that day. Having passed it, I know I can now use my next week to further my cause of earning my "Trail's Guide" qualification. It requires I must have at least ten VPDAs to finish the qualification. I must lead groups of people to View Potentially Dangerous

Animals in a way that follows the rules of viewing without endangering the group and without disturbing the animal.

When I return, glowing from the rifle test, Gerry is surprisingly still there. He is glowing almost as much as I am. He smiles hugely at me. "I'm staying," he says.

I laugh. "Don't you need to be at a tournament somewhere?"

"I can't help it," he says. "I love it here. I started driving toward the gate thinking how amazing this place is. I turned onto the N2 and was about a half mile down the road. I decided I couldn't leave and I'm not. I'm staying another week!" I laugh and high five him. *That* is *definitely* the spirit.

"How'd the rifle test go?" he asks. I almost burst into tears I am so happy. "I did it," I say. He is as elated about my success as getting to stay. Then something uncomfortably awesome occurs to me. Before I can really think about it, I ask. "Maybe you can come on my walk in the morning?"

"I would love that," he says. "I'll ask Pieter," I assure him.

I love the idea of Gerry Armstrong coming on my first walk, or any walk, but I have a bit of trepidation. What if I get the man killed? I have done over a hundred walks across Amakhala this year, but never one carrying the rifle and being responsible for everyone. That doesn't exactly comfort me, but having a legend be on my first walk seems too awesome to pass up. I ask Pieter. He thinks it is an outstanding idea. *The more pressure the merrier*, I know he's thinking.

The first walk goes swimmingly. *Too swimmingly, in fact.* Everything comes so easily to our viewing, the walk almost runs itself. I certainly didn't want anything dangerous to occur, but I wanted to do at least one thing exceptional in the presence of my new legendary friend. In the span of three hours we see our breeding herd of elephants, a mother white rhino and her calf, our submissive bull rhino, Chippy (who in 2010 would be poached), and

Nkosi, our dominant bull rhino, who, on my fourth walk, would give me the scare of my life. I log four views in one walk. I am nearly halfway there already and absolutely stoked. When we are through with the walk, I ask Pieter to allow Gerry to come with us again. He laughs. We haven't even discussed if I am going to get another chance to do another walk.

The next day we are up early for walk number two. I am again nervous, which I take as a good thing. The day one isn't a little nervous about leading people through big game areas is the day one's, or someone's, fate will be sealed. I check the rifle and go through all the necessary preparations. Pieter has decided that Erin is going to be my backup this day. That makes me extra nervous.

Erin has had a baby a few days previous, which is a testament to the same toughness that she expects of her students. She will grade me with great scrutiny. With my time greatly limited, I cannot afford to screw this up. Of the three possible teachers that could be doing this, she is the one I feel is the toughest. It doesn't matter in the end, I know. I need to get this done, and I need to do it right.

When all the other students Maya, Pam, Matt, Erin, and Gerry are assembled, I give the predeparture speech that is required before every game drive and walk.

"Everyone has everything he or she needs?" They nod at me. "Please stay in a single file, keep your voices down, and if you have a question or want me to stop either snap your fingers or whistle. If we encounter a dangerous animal please stand still, stay behind me, and do not run under any circumstance. Does everyone understand?" They all nod in agreement. I exude confidence but inside I am mush. I see Gerry's incredibly excited face and it actually helps calm me. I am going to be inspired by his enthusiasm, which is weighed against Erin's watchful eye. "All right then, let's go," I say.

I will have to balance safety and comfort and my desperation to find the animals. I know there is no guarantee that the animals will be anywhere near where I may be able to track them and I can't go into overly dense areas to find them. I have to find a member or members of a total of less than forty animals: elephants, buffalo, rhino, and/or leopard, (We are not allowed to walk on foot in the lion area.) within thirty square miles while walking with a rifle, five people, and at four miles an hour at most. There will be a lot of luck involved in this effort.

The .375 rifle feels heavy and cumbersome in my hand as we head out through the *Aloe ferox* at the back of the porch and into the reserve. I know I need to be in perfect control of it and aware of where it is pointing at all times. All it takes is one time for me to point it at one of the "clients" or Erin and the walk will be a bust. I also need to be in control of the group and my knowledge of the flora and fauna we see. I want to impress not just Gerry, but also everyone with the knowledge I have picked up along the way.

I radio out as soon as we are walking to find out if anyone knows where any of our big game might be. As we are up and out at the crack of dawn, there is no one to answer my call. *We're gonna have to do this the old fashioned way*, I think, as I lead everyone to the hill overlooking Impala Flats. Not seeing any of our Big Five on Impala Flats, I deign to look under the usual rocks where I know two different scorpions live. One, a smaller example of a *Parabuthus* genus, a very venomous and potentially lethal arachnid, and, another from the *Uroplectes* genus. Everybody enjoys them and my spiel about them, but being the head of a walking group is not nearly as fun as being one of the group. Even as we squat to look at the scorpions, I continuously sweep my eyes around in constant vigilance. I, as the guide with the weapon, am the first degree of separation between my walkers and potentially dangerous animals.

We cross Impala Flats and I am already sweating. The rifle, besides being heavy, is now wet and clammy in my hand. It is going to be a scorcher. I have to keep a watchful eye on everyone at all times to make sure everyone is keeping up, drinking water, and capable of not only making it out into the reserve, but that they also have enough to make it back as well. I watch Erin carefully from the corner of my eye. I know she would punch me in the head if she knew I was watching her or worrying about her in particular.

The other students and Gerry are excited to be out despite the heat and are enjoying the fact that one of the students is at the end of the program, just a few walks away from passing everything. At least that is the way it feels. Unfortunately, any screw up at this point might not just be failing but dying.

We reach Rooivalle, or Red Valley, called this due to its clay soil, about forty-five minutes into the walk. Technically the walk is only supposed to be three hours long at the most, so when I see Macauley and Bilike wrestling on the hill across from us, I am more than a little pleased. In fact, I would have kissed Pam next to me if it were appropriate. I look at the elephants wrestling one another and decide, as I am meant to, what is the best way to approach and view them.

I can see that the hill upon which they are wrestling has another hill behind Macauley, closest to us. We would be able to climb that hill and be right above and behind Macauley if he stayed on the hill with Bilike. I weigh the other options as well. I don't want to continue down the road and be beneath them. That would put us between them and the river. Although there is a lot of riverine forest to potentially find cover in, the total distance between them and the river they could cover in seconds. I reason the best way to do it is to climb the hill behind them and look down on top of them. I say as much.

Gerry's response is much different than Erin's. Gerry nods excitedly as I tell everyone the grand plan. The others take it in. Erin looks frustrated at me and says, "Absolutely *not!*" My eyes fill with anger behind my sunglasses but I don't say anything. "If we go up that hill right there, we are no more than fifty meters from them. We won't be able to see them and they won't be able to see us. If we make too much noise they may come to investigate and we'll have nowhere to go. I'm not doing it." I don't know what to say but know I better say something quickly. I certainly don't want to get anyone into trouble here, but I also don't want to treated like a moron. I realize I cannot argue with her.

I also can't tell if she is pretending to be a recalcitrant client as the teachers are wont to do for the purpose of learning, or if she is telling me that I am completely off here and going to get us killed. I know that Erin has a particular fear of elephants. This is due to a couple of bad experiences with elephants, including a hairy ordeal we had with Norman, our dominant bull, several months earlier.

Erin had been driving our Land Rover into the reserve through the gate. Once in the gate, there is a passageway with fifteen-foot sides made of tree trunks. This passageway is built so the animals can't race through the gate, as it opens slowly to permit vehicles onto the reserve. Just as we went through the gate, Norman appeared around the last tree trunk and entered the passageway. It would have been hilarious had it not been so dire. Our only recourse was to place the vehicle *as the gate* to keep Norman from exiting the reserve. Norman could have easily charged us and turned us into a garbage pile of squashed bodies and mashed metal. We all yelled at him and beseeched him not to come forward, none louder than Erin. Amazingly, he put himself in reverse and backed his enormous butt, head, and the rest of him out of the causeway. Erin did not love that situation as much as we did.

With this in mind, I decide the best thing to do is find an alternative route. "Okay then. We are going to walk back to Rooivalle and circle up and around where we will be able to look down upon the elephants, the river, and the plains. When we're there, we'll also be able to see in a number of directions to spot some more animals."

Everybody nods at me. "Great!" quips Gerry. Thank God for him and his cheeriness. At this point, I am feeling a little undermined and a bit of a failure. Improper approaches do not count toward one's record.

We clamber up and around to the top of Eland Point. I tell everyone to stay back from the edge of the huge hill and cliff. I will take a peak first to see if the eles are at a safe distance from the edge. I walk forward and find them fifty yards below us still wrestling. My eye catches movement to my right, two hundred yards down from me. A huge grin spreads across my face. *There is a God.*

To the right, on the plain not one hundred yards from the elephants, is a mother rhino and her calf. *Boom.* Two sightings in one place. It couldn't be a better sighting for a walking safari. The animals are unaware of our presence. Photos are perfect from the vantage point. Safety factor is at about 100 percent. In the span of ten minutes I have gone from worrying about failure to two successful sightings. I wave for everyone to come forward and let the photos begin.

I scan the area across the river called the Dairy for other signs of life. I can afford to be greedy in terms of having more approaches. Five more to go I reason. My heart lights up when I see another rhino mom and her calf grazing in the shade of *Acacia karroos* along the river. *Yes!* I walk over to Erin and point them out to her. "That's a little far don't you think," she says skeptically.

It is already 8:45 a.m. and getting warm. No matter how much I need this, I need to do this correctly and within the capabilities of my people especially the person who is grading me who just had a baby. I would obviously do this all day if necessary, as it is necessary, but I need to check with my "clients." I walk over to them. "Heh, guys. How do you feel? Can you do an extra couple kilometers across to the Dairy?" I point to the rhinos in the distance. Gerry bobs his head with his usual enthusiasm. "You bet!" Matt is in as well. The only one who doesn't seem thrilled with it is Erin and I certainly don't blame her. I don't want her to strain herself but I also know if I coddle her she might kick my ass.

I explain it to them before I put it to a vote. "All right, then. This is what we'll do. We'll cross over at the dam. Head up over the Dairy and then approach back from the west. Then we'll stop in the shade for a break. That work for everybody?" If I didn't have my sunglasses on they would all see the imploring I have in my eyes. I almost say a "*Yes!*" out loud when everyone, including Erin, gives the thumbs up. I am extremely grateful everyone is on board. I lead them across to the dam and up to the Dairy.

After twenty minutes of sitting, watching the mother rhino and her baby, and ruing the heat, I am pretty satisfied with the viewings of the day. There is no question that we need to get back. It is already 10:00 in the morning and approaching one hundred degrees Fahrenheit. I can see that the group has already backed me because they know I need it. I cannot ask them for more. Looking at Gerry who is completely unfazed, considering he has had to sit in the scorching sun a million times in his career while the world's best tennis players slugged it out, I make the command decision to take us back to Ulovane. I convey this to the group. As much as she doesn't show it, I can see Erin is pleased with this decision professionally and personally.

We cut across the expanse of the Dairy plain. We head toward the riverine forest directly across from where we had last seen Macauley and Bilike fighting but who we can no longer see. I take us along the shadowy treeline, stopping every now and then to listen to see if the bulls have found there way to the river and the trees. I don't want us to run into them crossing the river, or worse, in the thickest part of the forest.

I find a path that leads down into the forest and toward the river not far from Rooivalle. Erin stops. "I'm not going down there." I would start screaming if I thought it would help. Everything seemed to be going so well since the last time I got a protest from her. "Elephants go down to water religiously when it's hot especially after exerting themselves. They could be anywhere in here. We're not going down there."

I realize now that she is exerting her will rather than playing a role. I know Erin's will is not a malleable thing. I do not, however, despite her infinitely greater experience and knowledge, agree with her about the logistics. "This is the shortest path across the river and the only way across here. We either cross here or we're going to add another forty-five minutes to an already blazingly hot hike. Let's just go down bit by bit and listen every few meters. If we hear them, we come back and go to the other crossing."

Erin shakes her head. "I'm *not* going down there. They could be anywhere in there. If we stop moving, they will stop moving. They will listen to us and we will not hear them. I know elephants, Mat. I am not going down there."

I'm smart enough to know that arguing with her is only going to make my situation worse even if I do think she is being unreasonable. I look at the other students and Gerry. They are simply waiting for me to decide what to do. "The other dam it is." I acquiesce. We start walking along the tree line again.

Ten minutes later, we come to some shade next to a huge guarrie tree and stop for some water. Maya approaches me "I have to use the toilet." I nod at her. I remember the rule that when on foot and a client needs to use the toilet, it is better to retrace one's steps and allow the client to use a spot that has already proven to be a safety zone rather than find a new one with unknown hazards.

"Let me go back and check." I round the guarrie, walk back thirty yards and a little down into the forest. There is nothing there. I listen for a good minute but hear nothing. I look as far into the forest in every direction as I can but also see nothing. Maya will have her peaceful latrine area. I walk back to her. "It's clear." Maya walks hurriedly back in the direction from which I had just come.

We are standing no more than about two minutes when Maya comes around the guarrie with her pants wide open and her buckles clanking loudly against each other. "*Elephants!*" she hisses. I half raise the rifle expecting an elephant to burst around the tree in hot pursuit. She runs past us and looks back. "Twenty meters from me, just standing there silently behind a bush!" She zips up her pants and buttons them, a look of total consternation on her face.

I walk back twenty meters and look back. *How is that even possible? I was standing right there* shoots through my mind. I can't see anything nor can I hear anything as I peer into the forest. I know Erin is back behind me either smiling hugely or mentally deducting points by the millions from my score. I stride back to Maya.

"Are you okay?" I ask.

"Yes, yes," she says. "It just surprised me. I dropped my pants, looked up, and there it was!"

"I didn't see it. I'm sorry," I admit. "I'm glad it decided not to follow you," I add.

"Me, too," Maya says.

We cross the dam onto the plain adjacent to Impala Flats and begin the forty-five minute hike back to Ulovane. I am glad that I got the sightings right but am decidedly less pleased with my lackluster performance today in front of my legendary friend. Fortunately for me, Gerry seems to be as in great of spirits as when we started. Just in case I can redeem myself, I radio in for any other Big Five that might be available on the way back to Ulovane. There is nothing as all game drives are back in the lodges after the morning's game drives.

At the east end of Impala Flats, Lady Luck plants one on me *big time*. Up in the trees that separate the Flats with Platt, another grassy plain, is the family herd of elephants. They move among the trees, pulling down branches and making a general ruckus. There is nothing I need to do except stop us and watch them do their thing. I almost feel bad about how impossibly easy it is. Our safety is ensured and we couldn't have a better view at two-hundred-fifty yards from them. Although it requires no expertise on my part, I will get credit for the sighting. It is only a matter of explaining it to Erin when she goes over the day's events with me and my rights and wrongs. I look at Gerry and Matt, father and son, standing together as they admire the elephants. I am quite sure these two are as stuck on Africa as I am.

When we finish, Gerry thanks me profusely. I try to apologize to him for the apparent *faux pas* on my part but he is having none of it. He shakes my hand and can't sing enough praises of the morning, my knowledge, and my expertise. I ask Gerry to join me at Leeuwenbosch the next day, as I need to return to the lodge for another two weeks before the program ends. He agrees excitedly and tells me he can't wait. I can't help but feel I will always have a friend in Gerry, someone who seems to love Africa and its denizens as much as I do.

SIX YEARS LATER

I'm watching Roger Federer play in the semifinals of the 2012 Dubai Open on the Tennis Channel in Scottsdale, Arizona. I have been working for a year and a half now on my company TIA Safaris and Amakhala days seem a lifetime away. I am not loving being away from Africa for so long as the last time I was there was five months earlier with clients. Watching the Tennis Channel has helped pass the time when I am not marketing, writing, or doing lectures on African conservation. I write a poem about Roger.

Ten minutes go by as I am watching the live match and then a very familiar and welcome face appears courtside. *GERRY!* Gerry is supervising the tournament and, as his job demands, stands courtside making sure everything goes smoothly with the match. I can't believe it. I have not seen Gerry, even watching hours of TV when I was in Africa on the road, in almost six years. I immediately grab my computer and send him an email:

Gerry!

Ha! Ha! I just saw you on TV! Looking good my man! Look forward to hearing what's happening with you! Want you to know I'm writing my second book and I want to include your time at Ulovane with us!

Enjoy Dubai and give Roger a poem for me!
There is a guy named Federer,
a Grand Slam man go getterer.
We'd watch him play
all night and day
and we could not love him betterer!

Couldn't be worse could it?
My best of best!
Mat

Gerry shocks me by writing back almost immediately:

Mat,

If you see me giggling on the TV here, its because I've just read that terrible poem! Where in the world are you at the moment?

Over the next day as I watch Roger win the whole tournament, I pester Gerry with emails. Before the semifinals he writes:

Mat,

I was planning to read Roger the poem before the match while he was waiting to go onto court, but just couldn't do it. If I had, he would have been finished for that match!!

I respond:

Great Tournament Gerry!

No doubt because of your masterful dealings behind the scenes. Very pleased my man Roger won. Probably because of my brilliant poem making it to Dubai via the Internet! Are you coming Stateside for Indian Wells and Miami? Can't wait for those! You know I'll be texting you the minute I see you there on TV... Surreal experience really...:-)

Hope you're having as much fun as it looks like you're having!

Best,
Mat

Gerry writes me back:

I'm actually in transit now to Indian Wells, after which I will be in Miami as well. Send me a text, although I will try to keep hiding from you. Probably be asleep with jet lag courtside during the first few days.

Will be in touch from the desert.
All the best
Gerry

Once again I respond:

I hope you have a very safe trip to the States, with minimal jet lag. I was talking with my mom about visiting Indian Wells this year. I would love to see that tournament. It looks absolutely amazing on Tennis Channel's "Indian Wells" with Danielle Dotzenrod! Of course, it might just be because its Danielle Dotzenrod...

I look forward to seeing you giving Roger my poem on TV and you can be certain I'll be texting you in the middle of the matches...Ha ha!

Best of best,
Mat

Gerry returns my email:

Just overhead at the moment with a short stop in Phoenix. This has been a long day!!

Why don't you bring your mom and pay us a visit over the next week or so. Should be able to fix you up with some tickets, aside from the last few days,

Would be great to catch up and you could read the poem to Roger yourself.

Let me know

Gerry

I write back incredibly excited:

Gerry!

That sounds AWESOME! Would love to catch up again AND get to see all the best do their stuff live! Let me know what days work best for you. If you have the time (any time) we'd definitely take you out for BF, lunch, and/or dinner. I noticed you won't be running the show by yourself and have three helpers. Does that mean you have 75% more time?:-)

I think I mentioned it in one of the earlier emails, but I want to include the story how we met in my next book of stories (THIS 2 is Africa). It was such a surreal experience having the clash of my past failed dreams and present dreams (at that time) coming together at once when I met you. It will make a GREAT story! If you do have extra time, I'd love to pick your brain about your experience of Ulovane and Amakhala...Just so you know, the story won't work quite as well if I have to change your name...I will if I have to...

I'll even bring you and Roger signed copies of my book,

Looking majorly forward to this if we can pull this off...

Mat

P.S. Good luck with the jet lag. I don't know what works for you, but what quells my jet lag to and from Africa is eating at times that fit the regular daily schedule of where I landed...S--t, by now you must practically impervious...Best!

Gerry returns with:

Mat,

Let me know when would be a good day to come. Roger is probably playing on Sunday, Tuesday, Weds. Great matches all week so any day should be ok. Let me know asap when and how many.
All the best,
Gerry

As could be imagined, I let Gerry know very quickly. My mother decides that mahjong with her lady friends trumps seeing Li Na, her favorite woman tennis player from China. I head out to Indian Wells with only the hope of seeing Gerry, watching the players I only get to see on TV *live*, and possibly, if all the stars are aligned and Gerry is agreeable to it, having Gerry get my book to Roger.

"Get the book, Mat!" Gerry hisses to me from the door of the ATP supervisor's office. I look up from his desk where I am packing away my things in my backpack after a long day at the BNP Paribas Open at Indian Wells. I look at him, a "Why?" writ across my features. "It's Roger! He's right here! Get your book!"

I am riveted. I'm sure my mouth has fallen open but for some reason nothing is working. I almost think "Roger *who?*" as my brain can't quite wrap around the concept that Gerry is talking about the one person in human history I'd like most to meet: *Roger Federer.* I am a deer in the headlights. I've thought about meeting Roger Federer since I first saw him beat Agassi 6-0 in the second set in the Masters finals in 2003 and thought then he was the most ingenious tennis player I had ever seen. *A magician with a tennis racquet. An actual tennis deity...*

I shove my backpack aside and search Gerry's desk for the brown paper bag with my book in it. We had spent the last hour sifting through his unbelievable collection of photos of Africa on his computer he had taken since the last time I had seen him on Amakhala six years ago. The book is on the floor next to his bag. I grab it thinking, *Can this really be happening! Surely Gerry is joking! Do I even really want to be meeting Roger Federer!* As my hand closes on my book that I had given Gerry to give to Roger I'm more than a little confident I want to meet him. I jerk myself up and race for the door.

As I get to the door I stop to comport myself. I take a deep breath and tell myself, "Just remember, he's just another human being...He's just another human being." I round the corner of the office and there he stands, *Roger Federer*, facing Gerry, talking to him like he has done ten thousand times over the past ten years. My face breaks into a grin that would put the Cheshire Cat to crying shame. I take my first step toward Roger Federer and tell myself, *Don't you dare throw up on him...*

As I make the fifteen steps to Roger, I am gelatin on the inside. I think back to when I am stuck in Execution Valley on Amakhala with the angry elephants and I'm trying to show my clients that all is "good in the hood." *I was cool then and there was the possibility of death. I can be cool now. I don't think he's going to kill me.* That helps. I reach *Roger Federer* and extend my hand. Gerry introduces me, "Roger, this is my friend, Mat, he is a safari guide in Africa." I shake hands with Roger Federer.

"It is a pleasure to meet you," I say. "I've wanted to meet you for a very long time." My voice, fortunately, is measured and cool although it is taking every ounce of willpower for my smile not to swallow my head. Before I go into inescapable brain fart and forget my mission, I raise the package to Roger. "I wanted you to have a copy of my book. If you don't like it, your mom will. It's about Africa." He takes the package from me. "Thank you very much," he says with genuine warmth in his smile.

I hold up my ticket for the obligatory autograph. "Do you mind?" I ask.

He smiles again. "Not at all."

I watch his hand make his signature on my ticket like it is a magic wand. He hands me back the ticket and pen and says with a genuineness I somehow find surprising for a god. "I really enjoyed my stay at Shamwari in South Africa. They were just great there. We got to see everythi…"

"Oh, wow," I interrupt idiotically. I should not be shocked to hear Shamwari. It is one of the most popular private reserves in Africa, particularly for famous people, but I am. "You were right across the street from Gerry and me on Amakhala."

Roger smiles at my interrupting him and continues. "Yeah, we got to see everything. Today, I took my girls over to the zoo here to see the African animals. It was quite nice actually. They have all sorts of animals like those pig-looking things with the big teeth…"

"Oh, yes," I interrupt again, wanting to help and be as safari-guidish as possible. "Warthogs! They're great!" Roger is again very good-natured about my interrupting again. It is immediately obvious he is great at having people turn into absolute morons in his presence. "The girls really loved it," he says, obviously taking great joy in his twins having their afternoon adventure.

Gerry launches into the story of how we met and how I do all sorts of trips around Africa. He elaborates on his own trip, as I fall into a stupefied wonder at the fact that the deity I have come to worship in tennis terms is standing in front of me. I almost burst out laughing when it occurs to me to ask Roger if he would pinch me.

As I listen to them talking, I get the sinking feeling that I am supposed to be doing something. I have thought a thousand times what I would say to Roger Federer if given the chance. Now that I have my chance, I am absolutely *stumped*. I wrack my brain for what it was I was supposed to say to him if I had this very moment. *Nothing*. I feel the panic starting to build within me. *Calm yourself,*

Mat. Remember, you're a safari guide. You've stared into the eyes of a charging lion and not flinched.

Roger talks to both of us as if we were all old friends just stopping at 11p.m. to chat like we usually do. I recall a line by the always astute and perceptive tennis commentator Mary Carillo who said of Roger, "He has a quietness at the core of his being." I immediately have an even greater admiration for the man. There are at least a couple billion people on Earth that would love to be talking to him, a family waiting for him to get back to them at his Indian Wells residence, and he is here as calm as could be talking to some random fellow human being and Gerry who he chats with everyday. I just can't get over how cool, in the best way, Roger Federer unquestionably is. *Now, if I just think of what to tell him while he's busy being cool RIGHT IN FRONT OF ME!*

"Ah, yes!" I say out loud, interrupting Roger in midsentence. I realize it is more than a little rude, actually, more ridiculous than rude, but it comes to me like a thunderbolt. I know Roger has done some amazing things in Malawi by building schools for fifty thousand children with Credit Suisse Bank. Of all the things I could share, I thought this might be the most entertaining and poignant for him. Saying *anything* to him would be entertaining and poignant to me, but also given it's the one impossible chance I would meet him, I would definitely want it to be entertaining and poignant for him. So, after five years of knowing what I would tell Roger, I jump right into it.

"I'm so sorry for interrupting but can I tell you a story you might appreciate?" Roger looks at me with amusement or what could potentially be well-masked annoyance. Whatever he thinks or feels, he masks it like the champion gentleman that he has always proven to be. I cast a quick glance at Gerry to see if he is going to give me the hand across the throat message that I probably would not be able to adhere to even if I wanted. Gerry looks at me a little startled and with what appears to be "this better be good." Roger smiles politely as if to say, "*Okay, let her rip*."

"So, I'm in Malawi and it is the final of the French Open when you are going to potentially win your first Grand Slam and I would rather die than miss it. Problem is, I'm in a small village called Chitimba and the only TV is in Robert the Cool's hut and it is being used by a whole village of guys watching soccer. I know this because I ran to find Robert the Cool to find out if we could watch his TV. Robert the Cool is one of the carvers who sells his wares outside the campsite and who I have helped a great deal in the past so he feels he should help me in my plight. He says, 'I can't promise you that you can use it, but there is one TV in the community center and it is being used by all the children in the village to watch the same football match we are watching...' He can see I am utterly desperate so he takes me and a couple of my clients over to the community center, which is really a giant mud hut with a tin roof."

Roger and Gerry watch me with relative interest more, I think, to be polite as they are both, if anything, incredibly polite people, than genuine fascination. I realize at this point I just want to get the story out to accomplish what has been a dream a long time in coming to fruition that was never actually supposed to come to fruition. I plow on.

"So, we open the door to the community center and on the floor are about fifty kids whose heads all swivel around to look at we muzungus standing in the doorway. Robert immediately talks to the head honcho there who is watching the kids. That gentleman looks at the kids, back to us, and says 'Why not? The game is almost over.' He says something to the entire room of kids who look incredibly skeptical and then turns the TV to Roland Garros."

What I don't tell Roger is that the kids were immediately excited by Rafa if only because they thought he might be from African extraction, which Robert the Cool then asked me. I told him that he was from Spain but I'm not sure he actually ever told the kids that. The kids turned back to the TV and from that moment on they loved it.

"The minute the tennis started, the kids loved it! Now I can't say I loved it as it was obviously the match you lost quite 1, 3, and 0 (I'm actually cringing on the inside as I say this) but it was really amazing to watch an entire village of kids fall in love with a sport they had never seen before." I finish almost breathless.

Roger is an absolute hero with his response, something for which I give him almost as much credit as winning sixteen Grand Slams (At that time. He would later win Wimbledon that year). I can see he has almost no idea why I told him this story except maybe the fact that he can guess that I'd thought about telling him this story for the past five years.

He hesitates for a split second, and, wanting me to feel good about my story, says, "It's really all about the kids, isn't it?"

I could hug him both for his incredible generosity of spirit as his generosity in general. Hell, I could hug him just because he's Roger Federer.

I don't. As soon as I am finished, I am filled with a terrible anxiety. I have absolutely no idea what else to say. I know if I start asking him questions about life and tennis as Roger Federer, I might combust. It is Gerry who thankfully takes over.

"Great match, tonight, Roger. We'll see about tomorrow."

"Thanks," Roger says. He turns to me and extends his hand.

"It was nice to meet you, Mat."

I can't help it but an actual chuckle escapes me. "Heh heh heh. Yeah. It was *fantastic* to meet you." I shake his hand and can't help but marvel at the fact that he is a real, corporeal being. I'm actually embarrassed about myself but also don't really *care. Roger Federer* turns and walks away.

I turn to Gerry. He smiles hugely at me and I love him in that moment. He nods knowingly at me. I am barely containable as I raise my hand to high-five him. I stop when Roger calls out to me at the top of the stairs to the locker room below.

"Heh, Mat," he says. "Thanks for the book."

I look at him completely floored. *Did Roger Federer just thank me for my book?* "You, you, you're welcome, my man," I say. I didn't think I could have greater respect for a man of his genius, his generosity, or his geniality but I do. Roger disappears down the stairwell and I look over at Gerry, stupefied. "He's a good guy," Gerry says in his euphemistic way.

I give Gerry a hug and a high five. "I owe you, my man. I'd say there is no question I owe, you."

Gerry laughs. "It's the least I could do for you taking me around Amakhala." *No, my man, I think. I'm pretty sure everyone on planet Earth would agree, I DEFINITELY owe you.*

A PLEA FOR RHINOS: WHY WE NEED THEM

I am a safari guide in Africa. It is my job and life-sustaining privilege to share the beauty and wonder of this continent with others. People come from all over the world to escape the grind of nine-to-five jobs, the daily strain of civilization's demands, and of course, the restless, unquiet experience of twenty-first century living to revel in Africa's cherished and untamed wilds. My greatest joy in life is to see people experiencing these splendid wilds and watching as their restlessness turns to peace, anxiety to inspiration, and boredom to awe, to watch people irrevocably be changed by what they see in Africa, for the so much better.

In these wilds, there are certain animals in particular that fill people with this life-changing sense of awe and wonder. These animals reach into the deepest parts of our hearts and collective minds and are able to remind us of something *sacred* we seem to have forgotten in these past two centuries of mechanization, globalization, and technological advancement. Rhinos, both black and white, evoke this sacredness in people as much as any animal, as much as any *thing* on Earth.

Why people's eyes light up, why their breath catches in their throats, why they shift immediately in their seats to catch a better view or take a better photo, and why they will sit mesmerized for uncounted hours by these prehistoric-looking creatures, is not a mystery to me. A male white, or square-lipped rhino, stands over six feet at the shoulder. It can be thirteen feet long, and can weigh up to three tons. Its horn can stand erect from its face as tall as five feet. Its skin, making up 25 percent of its total body weight, covers the powerful pachyderm like armor. With its massive musculature rippling beneath its battle-gray hide, it can run up to forty miles an hour with the grace of a dancer. The sound of its breathing is how you would imagine a deity breathes. It is a creature bigger-than-life, perfectly adapted to thriving on the grasslands of Africa and would survive to grow to even greater dimensions, like its ancestors, if left to be.

Presently, the white rhino along with its cousin the black, or, prehensile-lipped rhino, are being slaughtered in Africa at a rate, that if something is not done *right now*, could prove to be the annihilation of these magnificent creatures within *ten to fifteen years*. With poison, rifles, helicopters, professional snipers, axes, and machetes, African and international criminals are making up to $50,000 dollars a kilogram killing rhinos for their horns. They are shooting rhinos from helicopters at night using veterinary-grade anesthetics. They are hacking and tearing the deeply embedded horns from the faces of these defenseless animals. They are then leaving the rhinos to awaken hours later to die a horrible, pain-wracked death from infection, necrosis, and trauma.

These criminals take the horns and sell them to the ignorant and uneducated masses, mostly in China, Vietnam, and Laos who sadly and incorrectly believe rhino horn has medicinal properties, curing anything from cancer to malaria, and magical properties as well. *It has none.* Rhino horn, made up mostly of keratin, is the same material as our fingernails. The only true magic a horn has is when it is attached to the proud face of a rhino brandishing it on the grasslands and in the woodlands of Africa, places that are becoming the killing fields of these noble beasts.

This proud vision is what our ancestors saw over a hundred thousand years ago, which inspired them to paint rhinos on the walls of caves and rock outcroppings across Africa and the world since. These artistic attestments to the splendor of these creatures show us now that our greatest grandparents believed that these animals were indeed, *sacred*. Our ancient families understood that all things had their place in the world, that all creatures big and small were interconnected, and that the extinction of one, like the rhino, may very well have meant the extinction of all. It is the very extinction of these sacred animals that we are faced with today.

In the wilds of Africa there are less than twenty thousand white rhinos and five thousand black rhinos left, a paltry scattering of the millions that once thrived across all of Africa. Why do we need them? The answer is simple. We need rhinos as we need *Wonder*. We need rhinos as we need *Awe*. We need rhinos as we need *Beauty*. Ultimately, we need them as soul-felt emblems of love for the very world within which we live. Charles Darwin once said, "The love for all living creatures is the most noble attribute of man." Letting rhinos in the wilds of our ancestral home, Africa, be slaughtered to extinction is akin to letting die this nobility that has been with us since the dawn of our time as human beings. Their tragic extinction would undoubtedly represent cutting us off, once and for all, like the proud horn from a rhino's face, from the *sacred connection* that we all once had to this living planet that sustains us. If we value wonder in our hearts, beauty in our lives, and an idea of the sacred in our world, we cannot let these magnificent creatures perish from the Earth.

Write letters to senators and congressmen, prime ministers and heads of state. Join or create an action group that gets the news out there. Use social media like Facebook, Twitter, and LinkedIn.

Give money to organizations that are helping rhinos like the African Wildlife Foundation, Save the Rhino Trust, and World Wildlife Fund. Best of all, for *you* and rhinos, come to Africa to experience their wonder, but please help them now, before it is too late for them, and us...

Thank you from the deepest and most noble part of me,

Mat Dry

ABOUT THE AUTHOR

M at Dry obtained his safari-guiding credentials from the Field Guide's Association of Southern Africa in 2007. He worked on Amakhala Game Reserve in South Africa for six months and then decided that he wanted to see more of Africa. In 2008, he joined one of Africa's premier overlanding companies, Africa Travel Company. For nearly four years he worked with ATC as a guide in both East and Southern Africa until deciding to create his own company, TIA Safaris. Mat now divides his time between educating people about Africa in the States, and taking clients on the trips of their lives into the Africa he knows and loves. You can contact Mat through TIASafaris.com or its phone number, 1-602-561-7823.

26983019R00142

Printed in Great Britain
by Amazon